The Hidden Life of The Prophet Muhammad

Dr. A. A. Ahmed

authorHOUSE™

1663 LIBERTY DRIVE, SUITE 200
BLOOMINGTON, INDIANA 47403
(800) 839-8640
WWW.AUTHORHOUSE.COM

First published by AuthorHouse

ISBN: 1-4259-0572-2 (e)
ISBN: 1-4259-0571-4 (sc)

Printed in the United States of America
Bloomington, Indiana

This book is printed on acid-free paper.

IN

MEMMORY

OF

THE LATE MRS. MATHAI

Contents of the Book

Introduction

It is very rare to find a book in the academic circles and public libraries that speaks about Muhammad of history. Most of the books today tell you about Muhammad of faith, the founder of Islam. In this book I am presenting Muhammad of history- his life, wars, and teachings. My accounts are based on the "Mothers of the Islamic Books ¹," the writings of the Egyptian Muslim liberal thinker, Sayyid Mahmoud Al-Qimni, and the views of some modern Muslim and non-Muslim writers. What is written in the "Mothers of the Islamic Books" is called "Al-Maskoot Anho" which means information that people- Muslims and non-Muslims - are not supposed to hear and know. Very few 'ulama "or Muslim Scholars" of al-Azhar al-Sharif University read these accounts and hardly speak about them even to one another. However, modern Egyptian Muslim writers such as Sayyid Mahmoud al-Qimni, Faraj Foda, and Nasr Hamid Abu Zayd endangered their lives by breaking the seals of these books and revealing to the public information about Muhammad that they have never heard before. For this reason Faraj Foda was shot dead in front of his office in Cairo, Nasr Hamid Abu Zayd fled out of Egypt to escape the death penalty, and Sayyid Mahmoud al-Qimni was forced to recant all his writings. Unfortunately before the outside world would get chance to read their works, these writers were silenced through murder, terrorization, and death-threat, and their writings are banned in the Muslim world. Besides that none of their books have been translated into English or any other western languages. In this book I am presenting the reader with the most important contributions of Dr. Sayyid Mahamoud al-Qimni. Accordingly, although many books are written about the life and teachings of the Prophet Muhammad, however, this book is unique because it reveals things you have never heard before and you are not likely to get them in any other biographies of Muhammad. No matter what religious background you come from, this book is going to change your understanding of Islam and give you better insight into our world today.

The Author: Dr. A. A. Ahmed. October 21, 2005.

Chapter One

THE ORIGIN OF ISLAM

In his book, *Al-Hizb Al-Hashmi Wa Tasis Al-Dawla Al-Islamyia (The Hashmite Party and The Foundation of the Islamic State)*, Sayyid Mahamoud al-Qimni[3] traces the origin of the Islamic religion to Abd Al-Mutalab, the grandfather of the Prophet Muhammad. "If God wants to establish a state, he creates men like these" said Abd Al-Mutalab while pointing his hand towards his sons" (al-Qimni 1996: 51). According to al-Qimni the idea of creating an Islamic state and religion goes back to the grandfather of the Prophet. Abd Al-Mutalab understood that the Arab tribes were impossible to be united into one kingdom because of a lack of tribal cohesion. In a kingdom, the ruling tribe would dominate other tribes and no tribe would accept that. For that reason the only way to unite the Arab tribes together was to have a King-Prophet to rule over them. Such a unity could not be resisted because it would be considered of divine origin. When he understood the problem, Abd Al-Mutalab borrowed the idea of the King-Prophet from the Jewish example of King David and his son, King Solomon. And so, he began his religion of Al-Hanafiya,[4] which he traced its origin to the ancestor of the Arabs, Ibrahim "or Abraham".

Furthermore, in tracing the origin of the idea of the Islamic State, al-Qimni went beyond Abd Al-Mutalab to the great grandfather of Muhammad, Qusay Ibn Kilab. In pre-Islamic period many Arab tribes struggled to control the important city of Makka: the tribe of Ibn Najjar took Makka from the tribe of Guraban, and then the tribe of Madar defeated Ibn Najjar and captured the city. From the Madar the control of Makka passed to the Yemeni tribe of Khazah. And finally the Qurashi tribe, under the leadership of Qusay Ibn Kilab, captured Makka. Through "deception, Qusay Ibn Kilab bought the keys of al-Ka'bah[5] from Gebshan al-Khouza'i, in exchange for a bottle of wine" (al-Qimni 1996: 81, quoting from Ibn Kathir, 194, and Ibn Hisham, al-Sira, pp. 109, 115).[6] When he took control of the city and the Ka'bah, Qusay founded Dar Al-Nadwa "or House of Commons" (Ibid: 82, quoting Ibn Kathir, al-Bedyia wa al-Nihaia, p. 192). Makka became under Qusay a small state and Dar al-Nadwa like a place of democracy for the Bedouin Arabs. According to Ibn Kathir, Qusay became a king and all the Makkan tribes became his subjects (Ibid).

The Ka'bahs: In those days Makka was not the only city in Arabia to have a ka'bah. There were the ka'bah of Najran, the ka'bah of Shadad al-Aiadi, and the ka'bah of Qatafan (Ibid: 65). Each ka'bah was erected to house an idol of a great tribal leader, known as Rabb "lord," or a holy stone. Volcanic and meteoric[7] "stones were objects of worship for the Bedouin Arabs. The Arabs venerated these two types of stones because the former erupted from the earth and the latter fell from the walls of the house of God in heaven. Richard Burton, who pretended to be a Muslim and visited Makka, took a small piece of the Black Stone and subjected it to a scientific test. The test proved that the Black Stone was part of the shattered pieces of a meteor (Ibid: 25). The Islamic myth has many stories to tell about the origin of the Black Stone. One story says when Adam was driven out of heaven he took a stone from Paradise and brought it down with him. The Stone was so bright and white but turned into Black because it sucks the sins of those who kiss it every year during the Hajj. Another story relates the Black Stone to Abraham and his son, Ishmael. It is believed that Abraham and his son used the Black Stone as a ladder to build the present ka'bah.

The Year of the Elephant: An important event took place in 569 or 570, known to the Arabs as the Year of the Elephant, which increased the important of the Makkan ka'bah (Ibid: 76, al-Suhaili quoting Ibn Hisham, in his book, al-Rawd, p. 77). The Ethiopian leader, Abraha made an attempt to destroy the ka'bah, but could not succeed. The Islamic myth said that heavenly birds called "Tair al-Aba'abeel" stoned the invading troops. However, the Egyptian essayist, Abbas Mahmoud al-Agaad believed that the army of Abraha was struck by small pox (Ibid: 76, quoting Al-Agaad, T'awal'ai al-Bi'atha al-Muhammadia, pp. 145-146). Al-Agaad drew his conclusion from the historical records of

3

the Byzantine historian, Procope, who visited Makka at the same time. The retreat of Abraha's troops made the inhabitants of Makka believe that the god of the Qurashi tribe had fought for them.

When Qusay Ibn Kilab died he left the inheritance of the ka'bah and the leadership of Makka to his firstborn son, Abd Al-Dar. However, his second son, Abd Manaf coveted his brother's fortune and tried to take the leadership from him by force. Al-Qimni found it to be unfair for the Islamic historians and interpreters to side with Abd Manaf instead of with Abd Al-Dar (Ibid: 89). The sons of Abd Manaf, Hashim, Abd Shams, Abd Mutalab, and Nawfal, wanted to wage war against the sons of Abd Al-Dar. However, the sons of Abd Al-Dar decided to keep the honor of their father by avoiding bloodshed and division and hence gave the leadership to their cousins. Al-Qimni expressed the attitude of Abd Manaf's sons in this dramatic way: "And the leadership which was taken by force from the house of Abd Al-Dar rested at last in the hand of Hashim, the son of Abd Manaf" (Ibid: 90, quoting al-Tabari, al-Tarikh, p. 123). As soon as Abd Shams died, his son Umayyah tried to take the leadership from his uncle Hashim by force. The Qurashi tribe once again prevented the fight when they sought the judgment of a Khazai priest. The priest ruled that Umayyah should be sent for ten years into voluntary exile. Umayyah chose to go to Syria in Al-Sham (The Fertile Crescent). The great grandson of Umayyah, Mu'awiyya would later on claim the leadership, which was stolen from his great grandfather, and he would establish the Umayyad Dynasty and wipe the descendants of Hashim from existence (Ibid).

Genealogy of the Sons of Qusay Ibn Kilab

Qusay Ibn Kilab

Abd al-Dar   **Abd Manaf**

Hashim/   Abd Shams/   Al-Mutalab/   Nawfal

Abd al-Mutalab/   Umayyah/

Abu Sufyan Ibn Hareb

Mu'awiyya

(Umayyad Dynasty)

Genealogy of the Sons of Abd al-Mutalab

Abd al-Mutalab

Abd al-'Aizi[8]/ Abd Allah/   Talib/   Abbas/ Hamzah

Prophet Muhammad/   'Ali (Shi'a)/   (Abbasid Dynasty)

<u>**Abd Al-Mutalab:**</u> After the death of Hashim the leadership of Makka and the Ka'bah passed to Abd Al-Mutalab (Ibid: 98). As soon as he became a leader, Abd Al-Mutalab began "to lay the foundation for a new religion in which all hearts could be united in one God" (Ibid: 99). He called for the abolition of idols. God would not accept any supplication from a person except his good works. God was the God of Ibrahim "or Abraham," the father of all the Arab tribes and the Jewish tribes. Abd Al-Mutalab had a vision while he was sleeping in the courtyard of the Ka'bah that the God of Ibrahim had commanded him

to dig the well of Zamzam[9] (Ibid: 100, quoting from Ibn Hisham, al-Sira, pp. 136, 139). Then he renounced all pagan worship and practices and asked the people of Makka to return to the religion of Ibrahim, which was the religion of Hanafiya. When the month of Ramadan came he would go to the cave of Hirah,[10] and worship. Abd Mutalab began to invite the people of Makka to do good and refrain from evil because he believed in the resurrection of the souls and their judgment on the last day. In fact Abd Al-Mutalab was not the first founder of the Hanafiya, but according to al-Qimni some people from Yemen founded the religion in the first century before the birth of Christ (Ibid: 111, quoting from Dr. Jawad 'Ali, al-Mufasal, p. 59, and Thuria Manquosh, al-Tawhid, p. 159). Abd Al-Mutalab did not know the origin of the Hanafiya and hence attributed it to the Hebrew prophet, Ibrahim (Ibid, quoting from al-Fakhr al-Razi). The Yemeni people used to worship one god whom they called Al-Rahman (Ibid, quoting from Dr. Jawad 'Ali, al-Mufasal, p. 59).

Many people accepted the religion of Abd Al-Mutalab and some of them made contributions to the new religion. The most important of those Hanifi[11] followers were: -

Qas Ibn Sa'ad al-Ia'adi who invited the people to follow "One God, who has not been begotten nor begot, and to whom all would return" (Ibid: 112, quoting from al-Shahirstani, al-Milal wa al-Nihel 1951, p. 96). Therefore, he was the first one in the Arabian Peninsula to call for Tawhid or "Oneness of God".

Suaid Ibn A'amir al-Mustalaq who said "man has no hand in what befalls him from good or bad. Everything was predestined by God" (Ibid, quoting from al-Awasi, Boloq Alarab, pp. 219, 259). Thus al-Mustalaq came with the doctrine of predestination.

'Awkia Bin Zohir al-Ia'adi who claimed to be a prophet (Ibid, referring to Ibn Habib, al-Mahbar, p136, and al-Awasi, Boloq Alarab, p. 260). He used to go to a lower place in Makka, climb a ladder, and tell people that God spoke to him in that place. However, 'Awkia was not successful in his claim to be a prophet (Ibid).

Waraqa Ibn Nawfal who called people to worship the God of Ibrahim and followed the Hanafiya in the beginning and then became a Christian. He was the relative of the first wife of the Prophet, Khadijah and through him, she confirmed the Prophet-hood of Muhammad (Ibid: 114, quoting Ibn Hisham, al-Sira, pp. 511-512).

Ala'af Ibn Shihab al-Tamimi who believed in the oneness of God, the resurrection of souls, and the reward of good and punishment of evil (Ibid: 115, referring to al-Awasi, Boloq Alarab, p. 277).

The Hanafiya followers used to practice "circumcision, pilgrimage to Makka, ablution after sexual intercourse, rejection of idol worship, belief in one God in whose hands are good and bad, and that everything in the universe is predestined and written" (Ibid: 116, quoting from Dr. Jawad 'Ali, al-Mafasal, p. 290). According to al-Qimni the only missing thing for the Hanafiya followers was the existence of a prophet

(Ibid: 116). When the Hanafiya people understood the importance of a prophet they began to compete among themselves, as to which of them was a prophet. They thought the prophecy would be revealed to the one who reaches a high level of spirituality and holiness (Ibid: 117). Therefore, one of those who was known for his spirituality was **Zayd Ibn 'Umar Ibn Nafil** who abstained from alcohol, eating of dead animals, blood, swine, and everything which was slaughtered without calling on the name of Allah or which was dedicated to idols (Ibid: 118, quoting Ibn Hisham, p. 206). Another Hanfi was **Umaiyya Ibn Abd Allah Ibn Abi al-Salt** who did not accept Islam because he expected the prophecy to come to him (Ibid: 121, quoting Dr. Jawad 'Ali, pp. 280-281, Ibn Hisham pp. 208-209, and Ibn Kathir pp. 206, 208). When he was told that the Prophet Muhammad killed the people of Makka in the battle of Badr he tore his clothes and wept and said if he were a prophet he would not have killed his relatives (Ibid, referring to Dr. Jawad 'Ali, pp. 377-378, 383).

Al-Qimni mentioned many poetic verses composed by these two followers of the Hanafiya, which were incorporated in the Qur'an (Ibid: 118-123). The following are some examples from the verses that Umaiyya Ibn Abd Allah Ibn Abi Salt had composed and were incorporated in the Qur'an:

About Ibrahim when he dreamt to slaughter his son Ismail, Umaiyya said, Oh my son I have given you as an offering to God, have patience that Allah may redeem you. The son replied by saying that everything belongs to Allah without exception Do what you have promised to do to Allah and do not look at my blood covering my clothesAnd while he was removing the clothes from his son, Allah released his son with Halal or "a permissible" sheep.

About Marry and her son Jesus, he said,

And in your religion for the Lord of Marry is a sign, foretelling about the servant Jesus the son of Marry.Descended to her after her people fell asleep, a messenger who did not confine or hide.He said, do not scare or disbelieve the angels from the Lord of 'Aad and Jariham. I am a messenger from al-Rahman to bring to you a son.She said, how can I have a son when I have not been a bad woman or pregnant or woman of high esteem?

About Moses and Aran and their story with Pharaoh, he said, Out of your goodness and mercy you made Moses a prophet. You said to him, go you and Aran to Pharaoh, who became arrogant. Say to him, have you made the earth without mountains to protect it?And say to him, have you made the sky without supporting pillars?

About the Resurrection Day, he said,

When they appeared before the Owner of Throne, who knows what is hidden and what is revealed.When we come to him, He is a compassionate God and his promise is fulfilled. And the sinners were taken bare-naked where there is their condemnation.There they do not die to take rest, and they remain in the sea of fire.

Quoting the words of Dr. Jawad 'Ali, al-Qimni states,

There is great similarity and agreement between the views
and beliefs of this poet and what has been mentioned in the
holy Qur'an regarding the description of the Resurrection
Day, Paradise, and Hell. More than that, we find in the poetry
of Umaiyya, the same verses and the same construction of
sentences appeared in the Qur'an and the book of the Hadith.
Of course, we cannot assume that Umaiyya had taken from
the Qur'an because the Qur'an had not yet been revealed. As
concerning his death at the ninth year of Hijirah, we cannot
also assume that he had stolen the verses of the Qur'an
because the Qur'an had not yet been fully revealed (Ibid:
123-124, Dr. Jawad 'Ali, al-Mafsal, pp. 384-385).

Along with the Hanafiya faith, al-Qimni spoke briefly about the
religion of Al-Sabiah or "the Sabians." According to him the followers of
the Sabiah "used to pray many times in the day and those prayers were
compulsory, they used to do qiyam (standing) and ruk'u (kneeling and
prostration), do ablution before each prayer, and wash their bodies after
sexual intercourse, and they have conditions that defile the ablution"
(Ibid: 111, quoting from Mahmoud al-'Agaad 1967, p. 144).

The Appearance of the Awaited Prophet: After this background,
al-Qimni said "and after that Muhammad (prayers and peace of Allah
be upon him) began to follow the steps of his grandfather Abd Al-
Mutalab to the cave of Hirah, and this cave was changed into a holy
place and entered history…and he believed in Hanafiya, and before he

reached the age of forty, he concluded the matter by declaring himself to be the prophet of the Umma,[12] after the God of Ibrahim was revealed to him" (Ibid: 132).

The people of Makka did not object to or accept the new religion in the beginning. However, the leaders of Makka began to protest when the verses of the Qur'an began to insult them (Ibid: 134). For example, in the Surah of the Qalam (the Pen), verse 68: 13, the Qur'an called Al-Akhnas Ibn Shariq the son of an adulteress because he described Muhammad as a mad man or bewitched person (Ibid, quoting from Ibn Kathir, p. 243).[13] In the Surah of Al-Muddaththir, verse 74:50, the Qur'an described the heads of the Umma "or community" as donkeys because they rejected the invitation to Islam (Ibid)[14]. In the Surah of Al-Masad 111 (The Flames) the Qur'an rebuked Muhammad's uncle, Abd al-'Aizi, and called him Abu Lahab or "Father of Flames," and described his wife, the sister of Abu Sufiyan, as the carrier of the wood in hell. And in the Surah of Al-Kafirun 109 (The Unbelievers) the Qur'an called the people of Makka unbelievers (Ibid: 135). However, the heads of Makka did not see the danger of the new religion until Muhammad started to stir the slaves against their masters. At this time the faction of Abd Al-Dar began to call their alliances from other tribes of Makka to join them in their attempt to prevent the new religion from spreading (Ibid: 141, quoting Ibn Hisham, al-Sira, pp. 238, 241). They saw now the sons of Abd Manaf trying to rule over all the Arab tribes through the new prophet.

The Alliance with the Medina Tribes: When Muhammad began to lose hope of gaining supporters in Makka he accepted the invitation of the Yathrib[15] tribes-Al-Khaoz and Al-Khazrig- to come and be their leader (Ibid: 150). The Yathrib tribes wanted to gain control over Makka by attacking it and preventing the caravans, which come from Al-Sham or "Syria" from reaching Makka. They would not be blamed for such a hostile action because it would be divinely justified (Ibid). The Jewish tribes, which also lived in Yathrib at that time, accepted the proposal of the tribes of Al-Khaoz and Al-Khazrig, and promised to fight along with them. Therefore, the verses of the Qur'an began to praise the Jews and their prophets and exalt them above all the peoples of the earth [see the Qur'anic Surahs Al-Baqarah 2: 62, Al-Maidah 5: 44, Al-A'raf 7: 157, and As-Saff 61: 6] (Ibid: 150). However, this friendly attitude towards the Jews did not last for long. The Prophet "was good towards the Jews sometimes, arguing with them another time, and had patience towards them until the chance came to pluck their fingernails (sic. i.e. to torture them), and finally destroy them entirely" (Ibid: 151, quoting from Ahmed al-Sharif, Makka wa al-Madina, p. 415).

As soon as the prophet moved to Yathrib, which he renamed as Medina, he made a pact with the Jews and began to attack the Makkan caravans, which came from Al-Sham or "Syria" (Ibid: 153). The alliance of Medina's tribes with Muhammad played a significant role in the defeat of the Makkan tribes. And eventually Makka fell and the Hashmi house took control of both cities. When Muhammad captured the Ka'bah the Arab tribes accepted the new religion (Ibid:

154). However, the victory of the house of Hashmi did not last long after the death of the Prophet. The sons of Umayyah, who had been exiled to Syria, waited for the right chance to take revenge on the house of Hashim. And when the right time came they did not only took control of the leadership, but destroyed the entire house of Hashim. They killed Hasan and Husyan the descendents of the Prophet and wiped the Hashmi tribe from the face of the earth. They even destroyed the ka'bah by catapult (Ibid: 154). Ma'uwiyah, the first Umayyad caliph uttered a poetic verse and that verse became the conclusion of the book, *Al-Hizb Al-Hashmi*:

> *The Hashmi tribe played with the leadership*
> *No report came or revelation descended from heaven* (Ibid: 154, quoting from Muhammad al-Qazooni, p. 9, and Ibn Kathir, al-Bedayia wa al-Nihaia, p. 227).

However, the story did not end with this an unexpected conclusion, but continued in Al-Qimni's next book, *Hurub Dawlat Al Rasul (The Wars of the Prophet's State)*.

Chapter 1 Endnotes

[1] For a list of the *"Mothers of the Islamic Books"* refer to the last two pages of this book. These books are approved by Al-Azhar al-Sharif University in Cairo, Egypt. Al-Azhar University is the oldest, largest and most prestigious religious university in the Muslim world. It controls the religious life of the Sunni Muslims around the world. 85% of the Muslims in the World are Sunni Muslims.

[2] The Chapters of this book are collection of Academic Papers I have written during my study of B. A. and Masters in Religious Studies and Philosophy in a Canadian University.

[3] **Sayyid Mahmoud al-Qimni** is a "progressive writer and Cairo University lecturer on Sociology of Religion." He is a PhD-holder from Al-Azhar Al-Sharif University, Cairo, Egypt.

[4] A monotheist religion in pre-Islamic Arabia. Islam is believed to be a continuation of that religion.

[5] An ancient religious shrine in Makkah, which is called the House of Allah in Islam.

[6] Following the advice of my Supervisor in my Masters, I will indicate in every quote the original source from where al-Qimni gets his information.

[7] Nicknamed Abu Lahab by the Qur'an (Surah al-Masad 111: 1).

[8] A holy well in Makka.

[9] The Prophet Muhammad claimed that the angel Gabriel appeared to him for the first time in this Cave and gave him the first verses of the Qur'an. In pre-Islam this cave was called "Khar Khirah," a place where the men of Makka would go to answer the call of nature. In those days Arabs had no toilets inside their tents.

[10] Follower of the religion of Hanafiya.

[11] Community.

[12] Qalam 68:13 "Violent (and cruel), with all that, base-born".

[13] Muddaththir 74:50 "As if they were affrighted asses".

[14] The prophet Muhammad changed the name of the city Yathrib to Medina.

[15] Ansars were the supporters of the Prophet who lived in Medina, and Muhajireen were those who immigrated with him from Makka to Medina.

Chapter Two

MUHAMMAD THE PROPHET

In his volume, *Hurub Dawlat Al Rasul (The Wars of the Prophet's State)*, al-Qimni analyses in details the wars of the Prophet Muhammad and the foundation of the first Islamic state. His analysis differs from the commonly accepted accounts of those events. He stripped the wars of the Prophet's State from any supernatural or miraculous nature, believed by most narrators to be the main reason for the victory of the Islamic State. Instead, al-Qimni attributes the victory to the successful leadership and military tactics of the Prophet Muhammad. Moreover, al-Qimni believes that the victory could also be attributed to the change of the Prophet's message in Yathrib or "Medina." Before the immigration from Makka to Medina, the message of Islam is based on a peaceful approach with full freedom of faith. It also admonishes the faithful to be patient and wait for their rewards in heaven. However, after the immigration to Medina, "all the followers of the Islamic community, Ansars and Muhajireen,[16] were changed into fighters and attackers, a complete State of soldiers and invaders, exactly like the tribe, and with its logic. This is after the allegiance has changed from the tribe and its worshipped ancestor to the State, which represents the men of war and blood" (al-Qimni 2001: 164). As concerning the change, which brought a sudden increase in the number of the Prophet's followers and led to the victory of Badr, al-Qimni states that

> And here is the most dangerous material change, which played a significant role in attracting the warriors from the weak tribes, after the Prophet remained thirteen years in Makka inviting people to his faith without gaining enough number from those weak tribes. At that time the invitation postponed the promise of enjoyment and abundance to the everlasting paradise…However, when it has been announced that Allah has given permission to the Prophet and the faithful to possess the wealth of the unbelievers, then the solution became an earthly and material fact, with other tempting gains before the weak among the people. These earthly and material gains attracted many weak people to join the army of the new State (Ibid: 165).

According to al-Qimni, the Prophet sought the alliance of the three main Jewish tribes, Qiniqa'a, al-Nadir, and Qurizahh, in Medina, when he was weak and had less number of followers (al-Qimni: 141). At that time, the verses of the Qur'an spoke "about the place of the children of Israel in the political history of the region of the kingdoms of David and Solomon, and their place in the religious history of groups of prophets from Noah to Abraham and Isaac and Joseph and Moses… etc., and that in great reverence" (Ibid). The Qur'an gives great and clear respect to the Jewish Torah (Ibid). At this time, the Prophet fasted on the Jewish Day of Atonement and used as the Qibla[17] for his prayers, Jerusalem, the holy city of the Jews.

Al-Qimni believes that the Jews of Medina accepted the alliance of Muhammad for what it might bring to them in the future in material benefits (Ibid). However, "the Jews of Yathrib, as they prepare themselves for the gains, they discovered, especially after the Battle of Badr, their deadly miscalculation. It became clear that the Muslims had gained in Badr material power and confidence, and therefore did not need that beneficial alliance" (Ibid: 141-142). As soon as the Prophet returned from his victory in Badr "he gathered the Jews in the market of Qiniqa'a and said to them; 'oh community of the Jews accept Islam before it befalls you what has befallen Qurash" (Ibid: 243, quoting from al-Bihaqi, p. 173). Although, the Prophet had given no choice for the Jews of Qiniqa'a except Islam or death, al-Qimni argues that the Islamic books of the sira[18] found justification for breaking the treaty with the Jews (Ibid: 244). According to the narrators of the sira, an Arab woman went to the market of Qiniqa'a to shop and a group of young Jews teased her and exposed her private parts. A Muslim man killed one of those boys and he got killed by a group of Jews. Al-Qimni refused to accept such a justification for expelling an entire tribe from

Yathrib and forcing them to go out of Arabia and settled in al-Sham or "Syria" (Ibid: 246, quoting from al-Halabi, p. 478).

The second Jewish tribe, al-Nadir, was accused of planning to murder the Prophet. Al-Qimni once again expressed his doubt about such an excuse for expelling out of Arabia another Jewish tribe after confiscating all their properties and wealth and distributing them among the Muslims. However, this time the justification came from heaven "as heaven informed the Prophet through its mediator, the angel Gabriel, that some of the Jews said to each other, 'you will not find the man as he is now,' and the messenger of Allah is sitting near one of their walls, 'a man should climb over the house and throw a rock on him and kill him and give us peace" (Ibid: 355, quoting Ibn Kathir, al-Bedyia, p. 76). After the angel Gabriel revealed the plan of assassination to the Prophet, the messenger of Allah raided the tribe of Nadir and forced them to surrender to him. The prophet likewise distributed their properties and wealth among the Muslims and allowed them to march out of Arabia to settle in Palestine (Ibid: 360).

The Slaughter of Qirizah: The Jewish tribe of Qirizah were accused of conspiring with the enemy at the Khazwat al-Khandaq or "the Battle of the Ditch". According to al-Qimni, the allies of the Makkans surrendered Medina and planned their deadly attack on Muhammad and his followers. When Muhammad knew about the allied troops, he dug a ditch around Medina to keep the enemy forces from attacking him. The only place that had not been protected was the area where the Jews of Qirizah lived in their strong garrisons. The prophet knew about that weak point but believed in his treaty with the Jews. While the enemy forces were surrounding Medina a rumor reached the Prophet that the Jews had agreed to open their garrisons so that the enemy could pass in and destroy the Muslim troops. Al-Qimni once again expressed his suspicion about such a secret plan between the Jews and the enemy. The Jewish leader of the tribe of Qirizah, Ka'ab, opened his garrison to the expelled Jewish leader of the tribe of Nadir, Huaya (Ibid: 383, quoting from al-Tabari p. 571, Ibn Hisham p. 261, and Ibn al-Athir p. 180). After long debate between the two leaders, Ka'ab agreed to open his garrisons for the allied forces to enter Medina and attack the Muslim troops. However, al-Qimni doubted such a possibility because the Jews never opened their garrisons to the enemy. For al-Qimni, even if the Jews had agreed to open their garrisons but did not actually do so, they should not be accused of breaking their treaty with the Prophet (Ibid: 384).

In tragic and dramatic details, al-Qimni narrates how the tribe of Qirizah were slaughtered mercilessly as soon as the allied forces left. It was Gabriel once again who instigated the Prophet to march against the tribe of Qirizah.

Narrated by "A'isha: when the messenger of Allah became free from the allied forces, entered to his house to wash himself for the prayer, Gabriel came to him, whom I have seen with his head covered by dust. He said to the Prophet; oh Muhammad, have you laid down your weapons? The prophet said to him; we put down our weapons. Gabriel said to him; we have not yet laid down our weapons. Arise and march to Bani Qirizah…

The messenger of Allah commanded a muzzein[19] to call on people, that any one hear and obey must not perform the 'Asir prayer except in Bani Qirizah (Ibid: 390-391, quoting from Ibn Kathir p. 119).

The tribe of Qizirah were left with no choice except to surrender to the Muslims and wait for their destiny. They expected the Prophet would do to them as he did to the other two Jewish tribes, confiscating their properties, cattle, and wealth and expelling them out of Arabia. Instead the Prophet left their destiny to be decided by an Arab leader, known as Sa'ad bin Mu'aaz. This leader suggested that all the men to be killed and the women, children, and the properties to be distributed among the Muslims. The decision was confirmed by the Prophet as he said to Sa'ad bin Mu'aaz, "You have judged on them by the judgment of Allah, which has been given to you from the seven heavens" (Ibid: 395, quoting from al-Tabari pp. 587-588). Al-Qimni continues, "And we learn from our heritage a new thing happened in that **slaughter**. The slaughter was not restricted to men only, but included small boys too" (Ibid: 398 referring to al-Tabari p. 591, emphasis in the original).

According to the narrators of the sira, Allah rewarded Sa'ad bin Mu'aaz for his decision and that by dying immediately after the slaughter. The angel Gabriel came to the Prophet in the middle of the night and told him that Sa'ad bin Mu'aaz died and the throne of Allah was shaken in his honour. Moreover, his funeral was attended by seventy thousands angels (Ibid: 397, quoting from al-Bihaqi pp. 28-29). Al-Qimni blames the narrators of the sira and in particular Ibn Hisham for adding supernatural events in order to prove a divine intervention in the slaughter of Bani Qirizah and the failure of the allied forces in entering the city. He says, "Although Ibn Hisham knew where the deception was, how it was planned, and who planned it in order to involve Qirizah with the allied forces, still he said with the confidence of a believer who knew for sure what he was saying that 'Allah spoiled their plan" (Ibid: 388). And this supernatural intervention is confirmed by a verse from the Qur'an, which says, "O ye who believe! remember the Grace of Allah, (bestowed) on you, when there came down on you hosts (to overwhelm you): but We sent against them a hurricane and forces that ye saw not: but Allah sees (clearly) all that ye do" (Al-Ahzab 33: 9). These angelic troops did not fight in the Battle of the Ditch as they did in the Battle of Badr, but they moved that strong storm which led to the defeat and retreat of the allied forces (Ibid: 389).

According to al-Qimni, the defeat and retreat of the allied forces has nothing to do with supernatural intervention. The Prophet understood that, as the Muslims had a weak point (i.e. Bani Qirizah), the allied forces too had a weak point and that was the tribe of Qatfan, a branch of the Fazari tribes (Ibid: 385). Through his spies the Prophet knew that the tribe of Qatfan joined the allied forces in order to revenge the murder of their wise woman, Um Qirfa, whom the Prophet killed by tying her to two camels and splitting her body in two halves (Ibid: 299, quoting from al-Tabari p. 643 and al-Suhaili p. 237). Um Qirfa was a hundred years old when she was subjected to such a cruel death, and she was murdered for no reason except that she was known as the wisest woman in Arabia (Ibid). Therefore, the Prophet understood that the problem of Qatfan could be solved by promising them some material gains if they withdraw from the allied troops.

> The prophet sent secretly to the two leaders of Qatfan, Husn and Haris bin 'Awf, requesting them to withdraw from the allied forces with the promise to give them **one third** of the harvest of al-Medina. The secret deal went on until the greedy, 'Ainiah put as a condition for the withdrawal **half of the harvest**. The prophet agreed to give **half** of the harvest with the condition that the leaders should create a division between Qirizah and the allied forces (Ibid: 385, quoting from Ibn Sa'ad p. 52, emphasis in the original).

Through secret deal and deception, a leader from Qatfan by the name of Nai'am bin Mu'aaz, who became Muslim secretly, was able to create a division between the allied forces and Qirizah (Ibid: 386-387). He convinced Qirizah not to open their garrisons to the allied forces because they live in Medina and that might lead to bad consequences when the Qurash and the Qatfan troops returned to their cities. He also convinced the Qurashi leader, Abu Sufyan bin Hareb that the Jews of Qirizah regretted their decision and asked the prophet to forgive them. They said to the Prophet "would it please you if we arrest the leaders of the two tribes, Qurash and Qatfan, and hand them over to you to strike their necks? Then, we will join you in the battle until we destroy all their remaining troops. And the prophet responded to them by saying, 'Yes" (Ibid: 387). Al-Qimni sums up his accounts of the battle of the Ditch and the slaughter of Qirizah, by quoting the words of the Prophet to Nai'am bin Mu'aaz, in which he said, "Deceive them for us if you can, for **war is deception**" (Ibid: 386, quoting from Ibn Hisham p. 265, emphasis in the original).

After the expulsion of the two Jewish tribes of Qiniqa'a and Nadir and the slaughter of the third Jewish tribe of Qirizah, there were no Jewish tribes left in Arabia except those who lived in the city of Khibar. The city was entirely inhabited by Jews. It had very strong garrisons. The prophet told his followers that he had received a promise from heaven to conquer the city (Ibid: 442, referring to al-Bihaqi, Dalaial, p. 197). As soon as the Prophet returned from the Treaty of Hudaybiyah,[20] he decided to attack Khibar. According to al-Qimni at this time the Prophet has fully turned from the Jews and their religion and began to incorporate in his religion the religious rituals of the pagans of Makka. Of that he says, "The Prophet knew for sure that the existence of Jews with a heavenly book, a historical heritage, and series of prophecies that followed one after the other, means the existence of continuous denial of his prophet-hood, and inside his city and in the midst of his small state. Therefore, followed those quick steps of cleaning Yathrib" from the Jews (Ibid: 367). Moreover, al-Qimni believes that the change had been noticed and appreciated by the pagans of Makka.

During this time all religious symbols of the Jews were put behind. The Makkan Ka'aba replaced Jerusalem. The Prophet began to glorify the Temple, which the pagan Arabs worshipped all their past history at the time of Jahiliya… This change drew the attention of the Qurashi tribes in Makka. They noticed that after the battle of the Ditch the Prophet got rid of the last Jewish tribe in Yathrib, and with the Treaty of Hudaybiyah, he turned his heart to the Arab-Makkan-Qurashi feelings. He accepted all the ancient religious rituals, which were their rituals and customs (Ibid: 437).

The Invasion of Khibar: Twenty days after the Treaty of Hudaybiyah, the Prophet led his troops towards Khibar. Khibar was the second city, after Makka, in its importance and military force. The Jews of Khibar had not expected Muhammad to attack them and therefore the sudden arrival of the Muslim troops was a great surprise to the inhabitants of the city. However, the city was well protected by its high and strong garrisons. For this reason, the Khibarians felt safe inside their strongholds and refused to listen to the Prophet's repeated calling to surrender to him (Ibid: 444). When the city refused to surrender, "the Prophet decided to use the catapults" to destroy the garrisons (Ibid). According to al-Qimni, the catapults had never been used in Arabia before that day (Ibid). When the garrisoned Jews saw the catapults, "they knew their death was near, and if the prophet strike the city with the catapults, he will destroy it to the ground and everyone inside the city would perish" (Ibid). In order to avoid such devastation the leader of the city, Cananah bin Abi al-Haqiq, emerged out of the city, holding the flag of surrender. He approached the prophet and told him about the willingness of his people to sign a peace treaty with him. The Prophet agreed on a treaty with the condition that "they should vacate their city and leave for him their money, garrisons, and land, and they should not take a yellow or a white thing except that which cover their nakedness from their clothes" (Ibid, quoting from Ibn Kathir, al-Bedaia p. 200). Moreover, the Prophet told the leader that if he hides anything from him then Allah and the prophet are free from that treaty (Ibid: 445, referring to Ibn Kathir p. 204). Al-Qimni also consults another Islamic source in this regard, the prophet said to the leader, "And if you hide something and I come to know it, then your bloods and women are permissible to us" (Ibid: 445, quoting from Ibn Sa'ad, al-Tabaqaat, p. 81).

When the leader agreed to reveal everything regarding their wealth and money, the prophet asked him about a treasure that he knew they had (Ibid). The leader of the Jews denied the existence of such a treasure. According to al-Qimni, the question of the prophet was a trap in order to make the leader fall in its snare because "the prophet knew already about the matter of that great treasure, and where it is hidden" (Ibid: 445, quoting Ibn Sa'ad p. 77). The information of the treasure had already reached the ears of the prophet through a Jew, "who sold his people and revealed the secret of that great treasure" (Ibid: 446). The prophet ordered al-Zibiar bin al-'Awam to torture the Jewish leader until he reveals the hidden place of the treasure. According to Ibn Hisham

"Al-Zibair used a burning rod and tortured the Jewish leader until the later died. However, the prophet asked Muhammad bin Salamah to strike off the neck of the leader and the neck of his brother Mahamoud bin Muslamah" (Ibid, quoting Ibn Hisham p. 43).

After the leader and his brother were executed, "the sword of Islam moved on the surrendered Jews, and killed from them according to the words of Ibn Sa'ad ninety-three men" (Ibid: 447, quoting from Ibn Sa'ad p. 77). The booty and the women of the Jews were distributed among the Muslims (Ibid: 448). According to "all the narrators of the Sira and the News, at the invasion of Khibar, the Muslim men forced the Jewish women to sleep with them openly, and the Khibarian women were shared by all men, until the Prophet stopped the rape of the pregnant women" (Ibid, referring to Ibn Said al-Nas, 'Uioun, p. 176). As for the Prophet himself he took Safiaya bint Huaya after he killed her husband and father (Ibid: 448-449, quoting from Ibn Kathir p. 197). However, at Khibar a Jewish woman, known as Zainab bint al-Harith, made an attempt on the Prophet's life and that by feeding him a poisoned goat at the house of Safiaya bint Huaya (Ibid: 453, quoting from Ibn Kathir p. 211). When the prophet questioned Zainab, she said to him, "you have killed my father, uncle, husband, and brother" (Ibid: 454, quoting from al-Bihaqi p. 257). Zainab was executed immediately. The poison remained in the body of the prophet for three years until it finally caused his death (Ibid: 454, quoting from Ibn Kathir p. 211). Therefore, the Muslims believed that their Prophet died as a martyr (Ibid: 454, quoting from Ibn Kathir p. 216).

The Attempts to invade the Roman Empire: Al-Qimni narrates in details the many invasions the Muslim troops carried on the Arab tribes, under the command and leadership of the Prophet. The military campaigns continued until most of the Arab tribes were subjected to the new state. The only city that remained out of the control of the new state was Makka. The prophet informed his troops that Allah had promised them possession of the treasures of the Roman Empire and the Persian Empire. In order to fulfill this promise, the prophet sent his military commander, Zayd bin Harith, with three thousands of his soldiers to Syria to invade the Roman Empire, and "the prophet knew exactly what they are going to face, and what would be the results" (Ibid: 469, referring to Ibn Kathir p. 241). When Hercules of the Romans heard about the approaching army, "he came himself to meet those who dared to come near the boundary of his kingdom, with one hundred thousands from the Romans and one hundred thousands from the Arab tribes that lived near his border and have allegiance with him" (Ibid). The huge army of Hercules killed the three leaders of the invading army and many Muslim soldiers. When Khalid bin al-Walid saw the defeat of the army he took the flag of Islam and withdrew with the remaining soldiers and returned to Medina. At the gate of the city the people threw sand on the returning soldiers and rebuked them for fleeing from the battle (Ibid. 470). However, the prophet corrected the people and told them, "they have not run away, but they withdrew for the time being" (Ibid: 470). The words of the prophet revealed that he still "insisting on the invasion of the Romans and Caesar" (Ibid).

After sometime the prophet himself went to invade Syria with thirty thousands soldiers and ten thousands horses (Ibid: 532). When the Muslim troops reached the border of the Roman Empire at Syria, and that Hercules the great leader of the Romans gathered a huge army at Humas to meet them, the prophet changed his mind and returned to Yathrib (Ibid, quoting from Ibn Kathir p. 178 and Ibn Said al-Nas p. 277). In order to find justification for the return of the prophet without meeting the Romans, the narrators of the sira blamed the Jews of a conspiracy. According to al-Bihaqi, "the reason which led the prophet to go to the Romans was a Jewish conspiracy... but Allah saved him from that conspiracy" (Ibid). The conspiracy was revealed to the Prophet through the angel Gabriel, when he reached Tabuk and hence he cancelled the invasion and returned to Medina (Ibid: 533, Qur'an: Al-Israa 17: 76-77). Therefore, the *promise* to conquer the Romans and possess their treasures and women had not been fulfilled at the time of the prophet. In fact the following hadith of the Prophet remains unfulfilled until today: "Invade Tabuk that you will possess the girls of yellow color and the women of the Romans. Algid said, give us your permission, but do not tempt us with women" (al-Tabari explaining the verse of the Qur'an in al-Touba 9: 49).

While the prophet was dying he sent his commander, Usama bin Zayd bin al-Harith, to invade the Romans at al-Sham or "the Fertile Crescent". Along with Usama, the prophet sent his two ministers, Abu Bakr and Umar bin al-Khattab (Ibid: 553). However, the two ministers, Abu Bakr and Umar understood that the Prophet sent them along with the troops in order to keep them away at the time of selecting his first caliph because he wanted 'Ali to be his successor. Of that al-Qimni wrote, "But they understood what the prophet had planned, and hence they objected to the appointment of Usama bin Zayd. Therefore, they delayed the troops at the Jiraph[21] until the prophet went to his Lord. At that time, they decided to cancel the mission and remove Usama from the leadership of the army" (Ibid: 556).

The Occupation of Makka: According to the Treaty of Hudaybiyah, there should be ten years of peace between the Muslims and the Qurash. When the treaty was signed the other Arab tribes were given the option to join Muhammad or Qurash (Ibid: 473). Therefore, "the tribe of Khoza'a joined Muhammad...and it was natural for its enemy, the tribe of Bakr, to join the Qurash" (Ibid). The enmity between these two tribes started before the treaty was signed. The books of Sira,

> Go back to a time before the invitation to Islam began. These books reveal to us the secret behind breaking the treaty of Hudaybiyah... They tell us that a revengeful enmity between the tribes of Khoza'a and the tribes of Bakr started when a merchantman from Bakr went on his way through the lands of Khoza'a. When he reached the houses of Khoza'a, the people killed him and stole his trade (Ibid).

The murder of that merchant led to a deadly fight between the two tribes and continued until the treaty was signed. A year after the treaty was signed "a war between Bakr and Khoza'a began suddenly, which our narrators blamed on the treason of Bakr... and the books said: the matter became worse when some Qurashi people supplied weapons to Bakr, and perhaps joined them in fighting against Khoza'a" (Ibid: 474, quoting from Ibn Hisham p. 84-85). When the news reached the prophet, he declared war against Qurash, and commanded his troops to be ready for the invasion of Makka (Ibid: 477).

When the Qurash came to know about the matter, "it sent its leader and the holder of its flag, Abu Sufyan Sakhar bin Hareb, to the leader of Yathrib" (Ibid: 475-476). The Qurashi leader requested the prophet to stop his troops because the Qurash has nothing to do with the fight between the two warring tribes, and that it still kept the treaty of Hudaybiyah. However, the prophet refused to accept the requests, pleadings, and apologies of Abu Sufyan. The prophet refused even to speak to the Qurashi leader. Therefore, Abu Sufyan ran to Abu Bakr and Umar bin al-Khattab and requested them to intervene to stop the war. When Abu Bakr and Umar refused to intervene, the leader ran to the house of 'Ali bin Talib and requested him to intervene, but 'Ali too rejected the request. Then, Abu Sufyan turned to Fatima, the wife of 'Ali and the daughter of the prophet, and begged her to intervene. Although Abu Sufyan pleaded, before Fatima, by referring to her son, al-Hussien, the daughter of the prophet rejected this request (Ibid: 476-477).

The leader of the Qurashi tribes continued to run from house to house in Medina until he finally met al-'Abass, the uncle of the prophet

Muhammad. However, al-'Abass said to him, "Woe unto you, accept Islam and bear witness there is no God except Allah, and Muhammad the messenger of Allah, before your neck is cut off. Immediately the leader of Qurash uttered the Shahadah[22] and became a Muslim" (Ibid: 480, quoting from Ibn Hisham p. 99). According to al-Qimni, the leader of Qurashi uttered the Shahadah out of fear for his life, but in his heart continued to follow his ancestors' religion (Ibid). When Abu Sufyan uttered the Shahadah, he asked the prophet, "What shall I do with my goddess 'Uzza? Umar Ibn Khattab heard the question of Abu Sufyan while he was standing near the tent. He answered him in a loud and mocking voice by saying, we will shit on her. Abu Sufyan said woe unto you Umar. You are a wicked man. Let me with my cousin, to him I am speaking" (Ibid: 481, quoting from Ibn Hisham p. 99).

Before he returned to Makka, Abu Sufyan wanted to save his people from the slaughter of the approaching troops of the Muslims. Therefore, he requested the uncle of the prophet, al-'Abass, to intercede before Muhammad to grant the safety of the Makkans. The prophet responded to the intercession of his uncle by saying, "anyone who enters the house of Abu Sufyan is saved, anyone who closes his door and remains in his house is saved, and anyone who enters the holy Mosque is saved" (Ibid: 481). Accordingly, when the Muslim troops entered Makka, the city was in full curfew. As soon as the prophet entered the city he went to the Ka'aba and ordered the removal and destruction of all the idols. Moreover, he issued death sentences on some men and women, who used to trouble or criticize him when he was in Makka

(Ibid: 487). According to the prophet's orders, those people should not be spared "even if they were found hanging on the curtains of the Ka'aba" (Ibid). However, due to the intercessions of some important personalities, some of those people were granted forgiveness.

According to al-Qimni, the compassion of the prophet towards the Qurashi tribes in Makka, was a great surprise to his followers, especially his Ansar or "his supporters" from Medina.

> Accordingly, the Ansar were astonished, and also Qurash were surprised, when they saw the prophet was restraining the hands of the Ansar from the people of Makka, and restraining the hands of the people from each other, declaring the sanctity of the House forever, releasing the people of Makka without conditions, and practicing all the religious rituals of Makka, even including respecting and sanctifying the Black Stone (Ibid: 489, quoting from Ibn Hisham pp. 94-95).

After the peaceful invasion of Makka, the prophet returned to his capital city, al-Medina, and there he continued to send his Sariha or "military missions" to invade the remaining Arab tribes and subject them by the sword to the new State. Therefore, the Arab tribes were left with no choice except to join the powerful state and save themselves from slaughter of the Muslim troops, and their women from becoming Sabaia, or "females taken as part of the booty of war." Accordingly, the year that followed the invasion of Makka was known as the year of missions (Ibid: 543). Many Arab tribes sent their representatives to declare their allegiance to the new state and accepting Islam. Al-Qimni concludes his book, ***Hurub Dawlat Al Rasul (The Wars of the Prophet's State),*** with the words of the prophet, which he uttered in his last days, "Allah has granted me victory through terror, and given me the plunders" (Ibid: 553, quoting from Ibn Kathir p. 197).

Chapter 2 Endnotes

[16] Ansars were the supporters of the Prophet who lived in Medina, and Muhajireen were those who immigrated with him from Makka to Medina.

[17] The direction where the followers of Islam must face when they perform their prayers.

[18] The books that narrate in detail the life of the Prophet Muhammad.

[19] The caller for Prayer or War.

[20] The Treaty of Peace, which the Prophet signed with the unbelievers of Makkah. According to the articles of the treaty there would be ten years of peace between the Muslims and the unbelievers of Makka.

[21] A name of a place at the outskirts of Medina.

[22] "I bear witness there is no God but Allah, and that Muhammad is the messenger of Allah."

Chapter Three

THE BATTLES OF THE EARLY ISLAMIC STATE

The battles of the early Islamic State were many. "The Mothers of the Islamic Books" give detailed-descriptions of every battle. However, in order to avoid graphic and horrifying descriptions of each battle, below is given a list of those hideous crimes that Muhammad and his followers committed against humanity and God. Muhammad said, *"I have been ordered to fight against people until they say that "there is no god but Allah", that "Muhammad is the messenger of Allah", they pray, and pay religious taxes. If they do that, their lives and property are safe."* (Sahih Muslim, #0033, and Sahih al-Bukhari, volume 1, #387, emphasis is mine).

Below is a copy of the message the Prophet Muhammad sent to the Julanda brothers through the intermediary of his Messengers, 'Amr bin al-'As al-Sahmi and Abu Zaid al-Ansari

Peace be upon the one who follows the right path! I call you to Islam. Accept my call, and you shall be unharmed. I am God's Messenger to mankind, and the word shall be carried out upon the miscreants. If, therefore, you recognize Islam, I shall bestow power upon you. But if you refuse to accept Islam, your power shall vanish, my horses shall camp on the expanse of your territory and my prophecy shall prevail in your kingdom.

623 – The Battle of al-Nakhala
623: -The Battle of Waddan
623 - The Battle of Safwan
623 - The Battle of Dul-Ashir
624 - Muhammad begins raids on caravans, Arab tribes, and Jewish tribes.
624 - The Battle of Badr
624 - The Battle of Bani Salim
624 – The Battle of Zee Amr
624 - The Battle of Bani Qainuqa
624 - The Battle of Sawiq
624 - The Battle of Ghatfan
624 - The Battle of Bahran
625 - **The Battle of Uhud**
625 – The Battle of Dumatul Jandal.
625 - The Battle of Humra-ul-Asad
625 - The Battle of Banu Nudair
625 - The Battle of Dhatur-Riqa
626 - The Battle of Badru-Ukhra
626 - The Battle of Banu Mustalaq
627 - The Battle of the Trench
627 - The Battle of Ahzab
627 - **The Battle of Bani Quraiza**

627 - The Battle of Bani Lahyan

627 - The Battle of Ghaiba

627 - The Battle of Khaibar

628 – 'The Battle of Humain.

628: - Muhammad signs ten years treaty with Qurash.

630 - Muhammad invades Makka.

630 - The Battle of Hunsin.

630 - The attempt to invade Tabuk

632 - Muhammad dies.

632 - Abu-Bakr, the first caliph, along with Umar, the second caliph continue the military move to enforce Islam in Arabia.

633 - The Battle at Oman

633 - The Battle at Hadramaut.

633 - The Battle of Kazima

633 - The Battle of Walaja

633 - The Battle of Ulleis

633 - The Battle of Anbar

634 - The Battle of Basra,

634 - The Battle of Damascus

634 - The Battle of Ajnadin.

634 - Death of Caliph Abu Bakr. Umar Ibn al-Khattab becomes the second Caliph.

634 - The Battle of Namaraq

634 - The Battle of Saqatia.

635 - The Battle of Bridge.

635 - The Battle of Buwaib.

635 - Conquest of Damascus.

635 - The Battle of Fahl.

636 - The Battle of Yermuk.

636 - The Battle of Qadsiyia.

636 - Conquest of Madain.

637 - The Battle of Jalula.

638 - The Battle of Yarmouk.

638 - The Muslims defeat the Romans and enter Jerusalem.

638 - Conquest of Jazirah.

639 - Conquest of Khuizistan and movement into Egypt.

642 - The Battle of Ray in Persia

643 - Conquest of Azarbaijan

644 - Conquest of Fars

644 - Conquest of Kharan.

644 - **Umar is murdered**. Uthman Ibn 'Affan becomes the third Caliph.

647 - Conquest of the island of Cypress

648 - Campaign against the Byzantines.

651 - Naval The Battle against the Byzantines.

654 - Islam spreads into North Africa

656 - **Uthman is murdered.** Ali becomes the fourth Caliph.

658 - The Battle of Nahrawan.

659 - Conquest of Egypt

661 - **Ali is murdered**.

662 - Egypt falls to Islam rule.

666 - Sicily is attacked by Muslims

677 - Siege of Constantinople

687 - The Battle of Kufa

691 - The Battle of Deir ul Jaliq

700 - Military campaigns in North Africa

702 - The Battle of Deir ul Jamira

711 - Muslims invade Gibraltar

711 - Conquest of Spain

713 - Conquest of Multan

716 - Battle of Constantinople

732 - The Battle of Tours in France.

740 - The Battle of the Nobles.

741 - The Battle of Bagdoura in North Africa

744 - The Battle of Ain al Jurr.

746 - The Battle of Rupar Thutha

748 - The Battle of Rayy.

749 - The Battle of Isfahan

749 - The Battle of Nihawand

750 - The Battle of Zab

772 - The Battle of Janbi in North Africa

777 - The Battle of Saragossa in Spain

WARS OF THE PROPHET'S STATE AFTER UTHMAN[23]

- <u>656</u>: Uthman is murdered. <u>Ali ibn Abi Talib</u> becomes the Fourth Caliph.

- <u>656</u>: <u>Battle of the Camel</u>. (Ali's troops against Aisha's army).

- <u>657</u>: Ali shifts the capital from <u>Medina</u> to <u>Kufa</u>.

- 657: Battle of Siffin.

- <u>658</u>: Battle of Nahrawan.

- <u>659</u>: Conquest of Egypt by <u>Muawiyah I</u>.

- <u>660</u>: Ali recaptures <u>Hijaz</u> and <u>Yemen</u> from Muawiyah. <u>Muawiyah I</u> declares himself as the <u>Caliph</u> at <u>Damascus</u>.

- <u>661</u>: Ali is murdered. Accession of <u>Hasan bin Ali</u> and his abdication. Muawiyah becomes the sole Caliph.

- <u>662</u>: <u>Kharijites</u> revolts.

- <u>666</u>: Raid of <u>Sicily</u>.

- <u>670</u>: Advance in North Africa. Uqba bin Nafe founds the town of Qairowan in <u>Tunisia</u>. Conquest of <u>Kabul</u>.

- <u>672</u>: Capture of the island of <u>Rhodes</u>. Campaigns in <u>Khurasan</u>.

- <u>674</u>: The Muslims cross the <u>Oxus</u>. <u>Bukhara</u> becomes a vassal state.

- <u>677</u>: Occupation of <u>Samarkand</u> and Tirmiz. Siege of <u>Constantinople</u>.

- <u>680</u>: Death of Muawiyah. <u>Yazid I</u> becomes <u>Caliph</u>.

- <u>680</u> <u>Battle of Karbala</u> and <u>Husayn bin Ali</u> is murdered.

- <u>682</u>: North Africa Uqba bin Nafe marches to the Atlantic is ambushed and killed at Biskra. The Muslims evacuate Qairowan and withdraw to <u>Burqa</u>.

- <u>683</u>: Death of <u>Yazid</u>. <u>Muawiya II</u> becomes Caliph.

- <u>684</u>: <u>Abd Allah ibn Zubayr</u> declares himself as the Caliph at <u>Makka</u>. <u>Marwan I</u> becomes the Caliph at <u>Damascus</u>. Battle of Marj Rahat.

- <u>685</u>: Death of Marwan I. <u>Abd al-Malik</u> becomes the Caliph at Damascus. Battle of Ain ul Wada.

- <u>686</u>: Mukhtar declares himself as the Caliph at <u>Kufa</u>.

- <u>687</u>: Battle of Kufa between the forces of Mukhtar and <u>Abd Allah ibn Zubayr</u>. Mukhtar killed.

- <u>691</u>: Battle of Deir ul Jaliq. Kufa falls to Abdul Malik.

- <u>692</u>: The fall of Makka. Death of ibn Zubayr. Abdul Malik becomes the sole Caliph.

- <u>695</u>: <u>Kharijites</u> revolts in Jazira and Ahwaz. Battle of the Karun. Campaigns against <u>Kahina</u> in <u>North Africa</u>. The Muslims once again withdraw to Barqa. The Muslims advance in <u>Transoxiana</u> and occupy <u>Kish</u>.

- <u>700</u>: Campaigns against the <u>Berbers</u> in <u>North Africa</u>.

- <u>711</u>: Muslims begin the conquest of Sindh in Afghanistan.

- <u>717</u>: Muslims attempt to conquer the Byzantine capital and fail.

- <u>732</u>: At the Battle of Poitiers, Islamic invasions are halted in France but continue into parts of Asia and Africa…

Chapter 3 Endnotes

[23] Timeline of Islamic History, 7th Century, "Wikipedia" Answers.com
http://www.answers.com/topic/timeline-of-islamic-history-7th-century

Chapter Four

CALIPH ABU BAKR AL-SIDIQ

Abu Bakr was the first caliph to succeed Muhammad. He is the father of Aisha, the beloved wife of the Prophet Muhammad. Al-Qimni discusses Abu Bakr in his book, *Shukran...Ibn Laden (Thanks...Ibn Laden),* under an article entitled "Apostasy In Islam". He wants to prove that apostasy was a creation of the first caliph, Abu Bakr, for the purpose of getting rid of those political rivals who opposed his leadership. Muslim scholars today argue that apostasy was based on an authentic hadith mentioned in Sahih Al-Bukhari. Therefore, Abu Bakr followed what the Prophet had sanctioned, which was the execution of an apostate from Islam. In this article Al-Qimni wants to refute such a claim.

The first source for the Muslim scholars is a Hadith in which the Prophet said, "Any one who changes his religion, kill him" (Qimni 2004: 202). This hadith was mentioned in Sahih[24] Bukhari and hence is for many Muslim scholars indisputable. The second source is a story in which the Companions of the Prophet killed someone who changed his religion. 'Umar Ibn Al-Khatab protested against the killing because the Companions did not feed the man for three days and ask him to repent before they killed him. The third source, which is even stronger for the scholars, is the famous Wars of Apostasy that Abu Bakr at the time of his Caliphate waged against some Arab tribes who refused to pay the Zakat after the death of the Prophet. Al-Qimni argues against these three sources and also against the new interpretation of apostasy, which was invented by some scholars of the Islamic Research Center of Al-Azhar University.

The New Interpretation of Apostasy:
Some of the famous and highly revered scholars of Al-Azhar came out with a new recommendation for apostasy in Islam. According to it 'if a Muslim becomes an apostate and leaves the Islamic Umma then his fate should be left to his guardian. If his apostasy does not cause danger to the society then his guardian must continuously ask him to repent throughout his life and in that case he should not be killed. But if his apostasy becomes a danger to the society then it is permissible for his guardian to kill him (Ibid: 199).

This new interpretation of apostasy contradicted the classic Hudd[25] of apostasy upon which all the founders of the Islamic schools agreed. The apostate for the Shar'ia law was understood as the state in which a Muslim man/woman left Islam and converted to another religion. Such a person must be given three days to repent and be killed on the fourth day. In the old interpretation the apostate was given three days to repent and come back to Islam or be killed on the fourth day. But in the new interpretation there were two types of apostates and each one was to be treated differently. In case when a Muslim left Islam and converted to anther religion and his conversion did not pose threat to Islam and the Muslim society, he would be left to his guardian to try to bring him back to Islam but not to kill him. But if the apostate became dangerous to Islam and the Muslim society, then his guardian should kill him. For Qimni this new interpretation was meant by the Al-Azhar scholars as a tool to get rid of the liberal secular thinkers in Egypt and to justify their crime of killing Faraj Foda.

The first source of the law of apostasy was based on a Hadith that was mentioned in Sahih Al-Bukhari "which is considered to be the most authentic book on the earth after the Qur'an" (Ibid: 202). Al-Qimni rejected this Hadith for several reasons. First, if the Prophet said the Hadith then why did the caliph Abu Bakr not refer to it when 'Umar Ibn Al-Khattab and some Companions of the Prophet stood against his Wars of Apostasy? (Ibid: 205). Moreover, if there was a Hadith like this then why did the Companions argue against the words of their Prophet? From this Qimni concluded that the Hadith was a later invention. Qimni likewise rejects the second source, which is based on the story of 'Umar, for the same reason.

Regarding the Wars of Apostasy at the time of the first caliph Abu

Bakr, 'Umar Ibn Al-Khattab said, "the caliphate of Abu Bakr was a mistake, that Allah protected the Muslims from its evil and that if any one tried to repeat that mistake must he be killed" (Ibid: 213). Must probably, 'Umar objected to the way Abu Bakr killed the Arab tribes who refused his leadership and the manner in which he was elected to the caliphate. According to the Qur'an the election of the leader should be done through Shura (every tribe should be consulted and its approval should be sought for). In the case of Abu Bakr many tribes were not even informed and those who objected were condemned as apostates and killed. Al-Qimni mentioned an incident in which the leader of the Khazrig tribes, who was very old and could not walk, refused to approve the leadership of Abu Bakr. 'Umar was annoyed with him and stepped on his body while he was lying on the ground at the time of the discussion between him and Abu Bakr. Yet another leader refused to accept Abu Bakr and travelled to Syria. Abu Bakr sent someone to kill him. Some Islamic sources said the jinn killed the man because he urinated on a wall while he was standing on his feet. Al-Qimni said many Muslim scholars today believe such a story.

According to al-Qimni the wars of Abu Bakr were meant to subdue the Arab tribes who refused to accept his caliphate after the death of the Prophet because they had not been consulted and hence they stopped paying the Zakkat. 'Umar and some of the Companions protested against those wars because the tribes were still Muslims and killing them would contradict the Hadith of the Prophet in which he said "I have been commanded to fight all people until they bear witness there is no God except Allah and Muhammad the messenger of Allah" (Ibid: 214). During those wars of apostasy the caliph's fighters "committed hideous crimes in which some Muslims were drowned in wells, others thrown from high mountains, and yet others burnt with fire" (Ibid). Al-Qimni narrated a story in which the leader of the troops, Khalid Ibn Al-Walid, one of those who had been promised Paradise, had killed the leader of Kana'a tribe because he had a beautiful wife. According to the story the leader and his men informed Khalid that they were still Muslims. In order to prove their adherence to Islam they told Khalid that they had just finished their evening prayer. Khalid ordered them to surrender themselves and lay down their swords and promised to negotiate the matter with them. When the members of Kana'a tribe surrendered themselves Khalid ordered his men to kill them. According to Al-Qimni the motive of Khalid was to kill the leader of Kana'a tribe and take his wife because she was a beautiful woman. Khalid slept with the woman on the same night he killed her husband and in that he disobeyed the Qur'an because he did not wait for the 'Ida time (three months and ten days). When Khalid returned to Medina, 'Umar met him and said to him "you have killed a Muslim man and taken his wife I swear by Allah I will stone you to death" (Ibid: 217). However, the caliph Abu Bakr did not consider Khalid to have committed adultery and hence did not punish him. 'Umar did not accept the decision of Abu Bakr and said to Khalid "you are the enemy of Allah because you have killed a Muslim man and raped his wife" (Ibid).

For al-Qimni, people like Khalid and Abu Bakr should not be

given respect because they were not worthy of respect because of their abuses. He further argued that those early wars were falsely forged and are taught to children in schools as just wars (Ibid 219). Those wars were political wars and meant to force the tribes to accept the caliphate of Abu Bakr, which in fact was forced on them. Therefore, any Muslim who protested against Abu Bakr's leadership was condemned as an apostate and deserved to be killed, his wife taken, his money stolen, and his children sold as slaves in the slave market (Ibid 248). The decision of Abu Bakr became "a horrifying and terrorist law even today in the Shar'ia which takes away the faith of people, reaches their necks, exposes their women, destroys their honour, enslaves their children, and robs them of their money and property" (Ibid: 250). No Muslim scholar was prepared to tell the common Muslims that "the great Companions of the Prophet protested against the Caliph's decision, among whom was 'Umar Ibn Al-Katab although 'Umar retreated from his protest when he declared that "I saw Allah has put the decision in the heart of Abu Bakr and hence I knew it was the truth" (Ibid: 251). Al-Qimni concluded that, "most of the decisions which had been clothed with divinity and became swords on the necks of the worshippers came as a result of those personal decisions. For example, Al-Bukhari included in his Sahih some Hadiths and rejected some Hadiths because his heart told him which were right and which were wrong. Therefore, al-Bukhari became divine and the author of a divine book which all the scholars agreed is the most authentic book on earth after the Book of Allah" (Ibid).

The new interpretation of the law of apostasy by Al-Azhar was meant, "to criminalize any scholarly research, forbid any new thinking, and therefore the work of the mind becomes forbidden, and when you research and discover some false sources for the Shari'a you become an apostate and the shedding of your blood is allowed, because you have discovered the falsehood of the law and the falsehood of the judgment and the judge" (Ibid: 252). Al-Qimni mentioned three recent incidents to show how the scholars used the law of apostasy to prevent other thinkers from exercising their views on Islam.

The first incident was the killing of the Egyptian Muslim liberal thinker, Dr. Faraj Foda. One of the Azhar scholars by the name of Dr. Mahmoud Mazroat said "any one who tries to prevent the Shari'a of Allah and wants the human-made law to be implemented is an apostate and it is permissible for the Muslim Umma to elect someone among themselves to carry the Hudd on him" (Ibid: 208). Because of this Fatwa and many others like it, which were issued by the Azhar scholars, Dr. Faraj Foda was murdered in 1992 by a group of fanatic Muslims.

The second incident concerned Al-Qimni himself. It was a Fatwa issued against him by the editor of the Islamic Newspaper, The Truth on May 8, 1999. The Fatwa stated, "Dr. Sayyid Al-Qimni dared to create doubts around the Shari'a in obligatory or necessary beliefs in religion which no believer would doubt except to become an apostate. He denied the Sunna of the Prophet and the one who denied it is Kafr or "unbeliever" by the collective agreement of scholars" (Ibid: 209).

Due to this Fatwa al-Qimni faced a lot of harassment and attack by the law, fanatic Muslims, and Al-Azhar scholars.

The third incident was related to a scholar from Al-Azhar who was not different from the Al-Azhar scholars in any respect. He was one of the best Mujtahdin among the Al-Azhar scholars. However, due to some of his new views in Islam "the state policemen raided his house and confiscated all his writings and pens because they have been considered as deadly weapons which threat on the peace of the nation" (Ibid).

Al-Qimni concluded his long discussion of apostasy by saying "on the ground of what we said, judging the person as an apostate because he denies one of the obligatory or necessary beliefs in religion, is nothing except a terrorist law, in the hands of terrorists, used by terrorists, and practiced by terrorists" (Ibid: 239). Therefore, Qimni considered the law of apostasy in Islam as a terrorist law meant to control and terrorize those who deny or reject some of the fundamentals of Islam according to the Shari'a schools. In fact many of the so-called fundamentals were not originally fundamentals in Islam because none of them was mentioned in the Qur'an or Sunna. They had been created by the caliphs and later Muslim scholars to justify the killing of those who disagreed with them. In that way they were against the religion of Islam itself.

Al-Qimni also blamed Abu Bakr, the first caliph, for refusing to allow the daughter of the Prophet Fatima to inherit the wealth of her father after his death. Abu Bakr claimed to have heard the Prophet said, "We, the prophets, do not pass our inheritance to our families" (Al-Qimni 2004: 242). No one else claimed to have heard this hadith from the Prophet except Abu Bakr himself. So, the only source for the hadith was Abu Bakr himself. Al-Qimni said sarcastically, maybe Abu Bakr heard the hadith when he was in the cave with the Prophet. In addition to the above Hadith, Abu Bakr narrated another one to justify his acquisition of or inheriting of the lands that belonged to the Prophet before he died. The caliph said to Ali and Fatima when they came to demand the lands of the Prophet as their inheritance that he heard the messenger of Allah said, "if Allah fed a Prophet He leaves it to the one who rises after him" (Ibid. p. 243). And the one who rose after the Prophet was Abu Bakr. Al-Qimni quotes a debate between Fatima and the caliph Abu Bakr, which was recorded in the Tabaqaat Ibn Sa'ad[26]:

Fatima: Who will inherit from you after you die?

Abu Bakr: My son and my family.

Fatima: Why have then you inherited from the Prophet and not us?

Abu Bakr: Oh daughter of the messenger of Allah, I have not inherited silver and gold from your father.

Fatima: And our share in Khibar and the lands of my father.

Abu Bakr: I heard the Prophet said; "We, the prophets, do not pass our inheritance to our families".

Fatima: Allah has said in his Book "Solomon inherited David".

When Fatima understood that Abu Bakr was not going to give her, her inheritance she came to the mosque and confronted him in front of Al-Ansar or "supporters" and delivered a long message which ended with the words "fight the unbelieving Imams of Kafur[27] for they have no belief until they repent" (Ibid. 244). Here she meant Abu Bakr and 'Umar because they refused to allow her to inherit the property and the lands of her father.

Moreover, Al-Qimni said Fatima died six months after the death of her father and at the age of thirty. She did not complain of any sickness and the cause of her death was not known. Besides that, the family of the Prophet did not know early death. For this reason, Al-Qimni suspects that Abu Bakr killed Fatima as he killed the leaders of the tribes who opposed him.

Chapter 4 Endnotes

[24] Authentic.

[25] Judgement or penalty.

[26] Tabaga'at Ibn Sa'ad is one of the most authentic commentators or interpreters of the Qur'an, Hadith, and lives of early Muslim caliphs and leaders.

[27] Unbelief.

Chapter Five

CALIPH 'UMAR IBN AL-KHATTAB

Muhammad died without seeing much of his dream comes true in raiding and looting the wealth, women, and children of the outside world. His first successor Abu Bakr likewise died without fulfilling that dream. The Caliph Abu Bakr spent his two years of caliphate in subduing those Arab tribes that apostatized from Islam after the death of the Prophet. However, in the time of the second Caliph Umar ibn al-Khattab (ten years) and the time of the third Caliph Uthman ibn 'Affan (thirteen years), the outside world was invaded and the Companions of the Prophet realized his dream.

During the caliphate of Umar, Muslim troops invaded many countries and reached from Asfahan in Iran to Triply in Libya.

1- In the Islamic year 14 Damascus, Hams, Balabak, and al-Basra were invaded and conquered.

2- In the year 15 Jordan was invaded and the Muslim troops defeated the Romans in the Battle of al-Yarmuk, and conquered the Persians in the Battle of al-Qadisia.

3- In the year 16 they invaded al-Ahwaz and al-Madain in the Battle of Jawala, and the Persian Emperor was defeated and ran away in the Battle of Yazidiger. In the same year Takrit in the east of Iraq was invaded, likewise the Muslim army invaded Qansareen, Halab, Antakia, Soroog, and Qirqasa.

4- In the year 18 Gandabsioor, Jawan, al-Rahad, Simisa, Haran, Nasibien, al-Mawsil, and al-Jazeera between Iraq and Syria were invaded and looted.

5- In the year 19 some lands of Caesar were conquered.

6- In the year 20 the Islamic troops invaded western part of Egypt and the city of Tastar in Iran.

7- In the year 21 Alexandria in Egypt, Nahawand in Iran, and Barqah in Libya were invaded.

8- In the year 22 Muslim army invaded Azerbaijan, al-Dinior, Masibzank, Hazan, al-Rai, and Asker and Qamwams in the middle of Asia, and Triply in Libya.

9- In the year 23, in which the Caliph Umar was assassinated the Muslim army invaded Kerman, Sajistan, Makran, and Isfahan.

In those bloody battles, thousands of innocent people were murdered by the Muslim troops. Many women were raped and many children were enslaved. Many houses were burnt and looted and thousands of families were destroyed. The Muslims robbed and looted the treasures of those places and distributed the wealth, women, and children among themselves. It is not a religion that they wanted to preach, but to rob, to enslave, and to rape. This reminds us of the teaching of Jesus about Satan in which he said "the thief (Satan) comes not but to steak, to kill, and destroy, but I have come to give life and life in its abundance." In order to know how much damage and destruction those Muslim Mujahideen did in those countries they invaded, read al-Tabari in his huge volume, al-Tarikh or "The History." One of those Muslim soldiers, an Arab man by the name of Mahafaz narrated one of his experiences in those battles. In the year 16 he participated in the Battle of Jawala in Iran. He said, "We entered the city and I saw a woman like a deer in her beauty and her face shines like the sun. I took her and her clothes and she became my jaria 'or slave girl' (al-Tabari volume 4, pp. 26-27).

The aims of those battles and invasions were not only to enslave and rape the women of those countries but also to loot the treasures. In few years the Companions of the Prophet became filthy rich that their wealth were counted in millions dinars. Just few examples would show how much those Companions stole from those countries they invaded.

1- When the third Caliph Uthman was murdered he had 'thousand of thousand' and five hundred thousand of darhim and one hundred thousand dinar. This is equal in our today counting million of dollars.

2- Al-Zibair ibn al-Awam had fifty-one thousand of thousand dirham and two hundred thousand dinar. Besides that he had houses and estates in Alexandria, Basra, and Kufa.

When he died he left behind him large garden if it had been sold it would have brought thousand of thousand and six hundred thousand dinar.

3- Abd el-Rahman ibn Awof when he died he left gold that they used axes to cut it.

4- Sa'ad ibn Abi Waqas left behind him two hundred and fifty thousand of dirhim.

5- Ibn Masood left ninety thousand dirhim.

6- Talha bin Abid Allah had in his hand a ring of gold, which has diamond in it. His daily income from his land in Iraq was one thousand dirhim or four hundred or five hundred dirhim annually. When he died he left two thousand and two hundred thousand of dirhim and two hundred thousand of dinar. Moreover, he left hundred jars full of gold.

7- Umar bin al-A'as left behind him seventy jars of pure gold. While he was dying he offered his gold to his sons but they refused to accept it because they believe it had been taken unjustly.

8- When Zayd bin Harith died he left behind him gold that had been cut by axes (Tabaqat ibn Sa'ad pp. 53, 76, 77, 157, al-Masoodi in Murouj al-Zahab volume 1, pp. 544-545, Khitat al-Maqarizi volume 1. pp. 140, 564).

The Murder of Caliph Umar: Umar used to warn his governors not to send any slave or a newly convert Muslim to his capital city in Medina. He scared that one of those who were deprived of their wives, children, and relatives might seek revenge in him. He called non-Arab people, 'Alwoj, which means dirty or unclean. So in every letter he ordered his governors to keep the 'Alowj out of his reach. In spite of his orders and fear, one of the so-called 'Alowj managed to reach him and take revenge for his family and children.

Abu Loloa, the Persian was one of the men who were taken captives in the city of Nahawand, Iran. The Arab Muslims destroyed his house, family, children, and his country without having done to them any evil. After he lost everything, he had been taken as captive to al-Muqirah bin Sh'aba to work as slave. For some reason al-Muqirah sent him to Medina. When he entered Medina he was grieved to see the children of his city and country and other countries filling the streets of the city. He searched with heavy heart for his children among them but could not find them. The crying of those wretched children increased his grief. According to Ibn Sa'ad, "Abu Loloa used to meet the children of captivity and whenever he saw them he used to cry and feel their heads with his hands and says, 'the Arabs ate my liver'. Then he killed Umar as a revenge for what he had done to the captives" (Ibn Sa'ad, al-Tabaqat al-Kubara, volume 3, p. 271). Abu Loloa murdered the Caliph Umar inside the mosque during the Morning Prayer. He pretended to be a Muslim and entered the mosque to pray behind the Caliph Umar. While the Caliph and the rest of the Muslims were kneeling in their prayer, Abu Loloa moved forward and stabbed Umar to death.

After this brief introduction to the leadership of Umar we return to al-Qimni and see what he said about him. Al-Qimni blames 'Umar Ibn al-Khatab, the second Caliph, for forbidding what is permissible in the

Qur'an. The Qur'an allows the believers to practice Muta'a (temporary or enjoyment marriage) (Q 4: 24), but the caliph 'Umar forbade and threatened to punish any one who practices it (Al-Qimni 2004: 236). And when the Prophet was dying he asked his followers to bring to him a paper so that he could write them a letter that would keep them from going astray. 'Umar said, leave him alone he is insane (Ibid). Besides that 'Umar was known, during his caliphate, for spying on people's houses at night.

The Umarian Pact:

When the Islamic troops invaded the Christian and the Jewish countries of Egypt, Jordan, Syria, Palestine, and Lebanon, the second Caliph, Umar Ibn al-Khattab forced the inhabitants of those regions to sign the following pact with the Muslim governors who ruled them: -

1. We shall not build, in our cities or in their neighborhood, new monasteries, Churches, convents, or monks' cells, nor shall we repair, by day or by night, such of them as fall in ruins or are situated in the quarters of the Muslims.

2. We shall keep our gates wide open for passersby and travelers. We shall give board and lodging to all Muslims who pass our way for three days.

3. We shall not give shelter in our churches or in our dwellings to any spy, nor hide him from the Muslims.

4. We shall not teach the Qur'an to our children.

5. We shall not manifest our religion publicly nor convert anyone to it. We shall not prevent any of our kin from entering Islam if they wish it.

6. We shall show respect toward the Muslims, and we shall rise from our seats when they wish to sit.

7. We shall not seek to resemble the Muslims by imitating any of their garments, the qalansuwa, the turban, footwear, or the parting of the hair. We shall not speak as they do, nor shall we adopt their kunyas.

8. We shall not mount on saddles, nor shall we gird swords nor bear any kind of arms nor carry them on our- persons.

9. We shall not engrave Arabic inscriptions on our seals.

10. We shall not sell fermented drinks.

11. We shall clip the fronts of our heads.

12. We shall always dress in the same way wherever we may be, and we shall bind the zunar round our waists

13. We shall not display our crosses or our books in the roads or markets of the Muslims. We shall use only clappers in our churches very softly. We shall not raise our voices when following our dead. We shall not show lights on any of the roads of the Muslims or in their markets. We shall not bury our dead near the Muslims.

14. We shall not take slaves who have been allotted to Muslims.

15. We shall not build houses overtopping the houses of the Muslims.

16. (When I brought the letter to Umar, may God be pleased with him, he added, "We shall not strike a Muslim.")

17. We accept these conditions for ourselves and for the people of our community, and in return we receive safe-conduct.

18. If we in any way violate these undertakings for which we ourselves stand surety, we forfeit our covenant [dhimma], and we become liable to the penalties for contumacy and sedition.

19. Umar Ibn al-Khattab replied: Sign what they ask, but add two clauses and impose them in addition to those, which they have undertaken. They are: "They shall not buy anyone made prisoner by the Muslims," and "Whoever strikes a Muslim with deliberate intent shall forfeit the protection of this pact."

'Umar Ibn al-Khatab is known among the Islamic circles as the most just judge and ruler that ever walked on the surface of the earth. For this reason he is called 'Umar al-Farooq" which means 'Umar the just.' However, the above "Umarian Pact" does not confirm his justice. Quoting Ibn Kathir, al-Qimni narrates a case to show how 'Umar deals with legal matters concerning the accusation of adultery.

It is an important case, which shows the attitude of Umar Ibn al-Khattab toward implementing the law of stoning in case of adultery… It is the most famous historical story in the history of the Arabs. It happened in the year 17 of the Higrah "or immigration." There is no Islamic book that does not include that story. Three important Companions of the Prophet - Abi Bikra, Nafi'a bin al-Harith, and Shibal bin Ma'abad- testified before 'Umar Ibn al-Khattab that **they saw al-Muqirah bin Sha'aba doing it to Um Jamil as**

al-Mail goes inside al-Mukahal. The three Companions testified to this act of adultery without fear or shame. When the forth Companion came, Zaiad ibn Shamalah, the Caliph Umar made him to understand his desire not to disappoint al-Muqirah bin Sha'aba. Then he asked him what he saw. He said **I saw them, and heard heavy breathing, and I saw him lying on her stomach and chest**. Umar said, have you seen him inserting it and removing it as the al-Mail goes inside al-Mukahal? He said, "No". **But I saw him lifting up her legs and his body goes up and down between her thighs**. And I saw he is doing that with full strength and I heard loud breathing. Umar asked, have you seen him inserting it and removing it as the al-Mail goes inside al-Mukahal? He said "No." Umar said, **Allahu Akabar**,[28] arise al-Muqirah and give each of the three witnesses eighty lashes (Ibid: 2001, quoting from Ibn Kathir, al-Bedyia wa al-Nihaia, pp. 83-84, emphasis in the original).

In order to prove the accusation of adultery in Islam there must be four witnesses who should testify in court that they have seen the adulterer and the adulteress in the very act of adultery. Before 'Aisha, the beloved wife of Muhammad was accused of committing adultery with the handsome young Muslim man, Safwan bin Al-Muattal As-Sulami, adultery could be proved by the testimony of two Muslim men or one man and two women. However, after the case of 'Aisha and Safwan the Qur'an increased the number to four men.[29]

"And those who accuse honorable women but bring not four witnesses, scourge them (with) eighty stripes and never (afterward) accept their testimony - They indeed are evil-doers" (Qur'an an-Nur 24: 4).

Nevertheless, after the case of **al-Muqirah bin Sha'aba and Um Jamil,** the Caliph Umar ibn al-Khattab **introduced the thread as an important method for proving the accusation**. Accordingly, besides four witnesses, the Shari'a requires that the witnesses should bring a thread and pass it between the adulterer and the adulteress. If the thread could not pass between them then that proves the man's penis is inside the woman's vagina. That is exactly what the Caliph Umar required from the four witnesses who caught **al-Muqirah bin Sha'aba and Um Jamil in the very act of adultery.** Basing their argument in this incident the Muslim scholars argue that Islam is the religion of mercy and that Umar was the just judge that ever walked on the surface of the earth planet!?

Chapter 5 Endnotes

[28] God is great.

[29] Please refer to page 131 under "Aisha accused of adultery."

Chapter Six

CALIPH UTHMAN IBN 'AFFAN

Uthman was the third caliph among the so-called rightly guided caliphs, Abu Bakr, Umar, Uthman, and 'Ali. In his book, *Rab Al-Zaman (The Lord of Times),* under an article entitled "We should not spoil our history and must have some wisdom and conscience" Al-Qimni corrected the claim that a Jew by the name of Ibn Saba was behind the murder of caliph Uthman Ibn 'Affan (Ibid: 105). According to him Ibn Saba was innocent of the blood of Uthman. The caliph Uthman himself was to be blamed for his assassination. Al-Qimni asked "if the Islamic state had become the greatest state in the world at the time of the third caliph, and the man had implemented the Shari'a and the Hudud, and established all the rituals and the rules of Islam, then why had he been killed?" (Al-Qimni 1996: 105). Al-Qimni responded to an Islamic article published in Al-Ihram newspaper, which stated "at the time of Uthman there was abundance of wealth in the Medina until the jariya (female slave) was sold for a quantity of gold equals to her weight" (Ibid 107). According to Al-Qimni, the master of the beautiful Jariya had been given such big price for the duty that she would perform in bed. However, the most important question for Al-Qimni was: from where did such an enormous amount of gold come? In answering this question, al-Qimni said, "the gold came from those countries that Muslim troops invaded and looted. Before that gold was accumulated in the hand of the buyer of the beautiful Jariya, it was scattered in the price of a goat of a poor Egyptian farmer, in the grain of an Iraqi who lived in a hut, and in the sheep of a Syrian who grazed his sheep in the wilderness" (Ibid). In other words, the Muslim troops robbed the cattle and the grain of the poor shepherds, farmers, and workers in those countries they invaded in the name of Islam. The looted cattle and grain brought to Medina and sold and the price was used as gold to buy the beautiful jawari or "female slaves". Therefore, the sweat of the Egyptian farmers, the Iraqi merchants, and the Syrian shepherds was gathered and sold and "poured in one scale and on the other scale stood a pretty Jariya" (Ibid). The books of Islamic history mentioned that "one of the companions of the Prophet left behind him more than five million dinars when he died and another one left gold that needed to be cut with axes" (Ibid).

The caliph Uthman was known for his nepotism. He took money from the Muslim treasury and bribed those who opposed his rule (Ibid). He sent two of the revered companions of the Prophet –Aba

Zar al-Jaifari and Yasir Ibn Amar- into exile because they reproached his behavior (Ibid). Before he sent him to exile, Uthman trampled Yasir under his feet until Yasir lost his consciousness. Yasir was one of those whom the Prophet promised Paradise. Uthman made Ibn Abi al-Sarah governor of Egypt whereas all Muslims at that time knew there was a verse in the Qur'an that was interpreted as condemning Ibn Abi al-Sarah to unbelief. Al-Qimni did not mention the verse but must probably he was relying on the commentators of the Qur'an. I will mention here a few names from a big list of the sources that he referred to in most of his books. In fact, in all his writings, Al-Qimni quotes from well-known authors of the so-called Umaha'at al-Kutob al-Islamia or "Mothers of the Islamic Books" such as Ibn Kathir, al-Tabari, Ibn Sa'ad, Al-Qortobi (known as Sheikh of the interpreters), Al-Sira Al-Halabia, Sirat Ibn Hisham, Sahih Al-Bukhari, and Sahih Muslim. In his famous trial of his book, <u>Rab Al-Zaman (The Lord of This Time)</u>, the court could not condemn him because everything he mentioned was well documented from those sources, which are accepted by Al-Azhar University.

Returning to the story of Uthman, al-Qimni continued to say when some of the Egyptians came to Medina and complained to Uthman about Ibn Abi al-Sarah, Uthman scourged them and killed one of them. Uthman also appointed his half brother Al-Walid Ibn Agaba a governor of Kufa when Muslims knew that this man had cheated the Prophet and had become an apostate after the death of the Prophet. Al-Walid Ibn Agaba used to lead Muslims in prayer in Kufa while he was fully drunk (Ibid 109). The un-Islamic behavior of Al-Walid led Ibn Al-Ashtar to rebuke Uthman in harsh words "from Malik Ibn al-Harith to the caliph who was corrupt, sinful, despiser of his Prophet's Sunna, and denouncer of the Qur'anic rule behind his back, keep from us your Walid and Sa'ad and every one whom your whims led you to send to us from your house" (Ibid 108).

The revolt of Egypt was encouraged by Mohammad Ibn Abi Huzifa, Mohammad Ibn Abi Bakr al-Sadiq (the son of the second caliph), and Yasir Ibn Amar (Ibid 109). Those three companions of the Prophet traveled from Medina to Egypt to move the people against Uthman. In addition to all these actions, Uthman also collected the Masahif or "copies of the Qur'an" (Ibid: 109-110). There were many different Masahif at the time of Uthman, which had different arrangements of Surahs and some of them included different verses. To mention a few, there were the Musahaf of 'A'isha, of Hafsa, of Ali, and of Ibn Masood. Uthman burnt all except that of Hafsa the daughter of Abu Bakr the second caliph[30]. This action led "the revered companion and the beloved of the Prophet, Ibn Masood to protest against what Uthman was doing with the words of Allah" (Ibid: 110). In response Uthman cast him out of the mosque and ordered him to be beaten until his ribs were broken (Ibid). Ali Ibn Abi Talib, the fourth caliph and the husband of the Prophet's daughter, Fatima, refused to surrender his Musahaf but Uthman took it from him by force. Al-Qimni concluded the article by asking "what was the role of Ibn Saba'a in this, and who went against God?" (Ibid: 110). What Al-Qimni meant to say was that

Uthman's corruption, nepotism, and bad rule brought the calamity on him and ultimately resulted in his assassination.

Chapter 6 Endnotes

[30] Please refer to Al-Qimni's discussion of Nasikh and Mansookh.

Chapter Seven

NASIKH AND MANSUKH

In his book, *Al-Islamiat (The Islamism)*, Al-Qimni begins his discussion of Nasikh and Mansukh "or the theory of Abrogation" in the Qur'an by referring to the story of the Satanic Verses (Al-Qimni 2001: 563). According to Al-Qimni the Prophet Muhammad wished that God should not reveal to him anything that might cause the inhabitants of Makka to reject him. While the Prophet, some of his followers, and the leaders of Qurashi tribe were praying in the Holy Mosque, he received a revelation from Allah which he read loudly as follows

[19] Have ye seen Lat, and 'Uzza,
[20] And another, the Third (goddess), Manat? (An-Najm 53: 19-20) [Yusif 'Ali's translation].

The Prophet continued to recite,

"They are the highest goddesses (or intercessors) and their intercession should be sought for" (emphasis is mine).

[31]When Muhammad read those verses "no one remained in the Mosque either Muslim or Kafir or "unbeliever" who had not prostrated along with the Prophet" (Ibid). Then Muhammad said the angel Gabriel came and rebuked him and told him that he had read to people what he had not revealed to him.

[73] "And their purpose was to tempt thee away from that which We had revealed unto thee, to substitute in Our name something quite different: (in that case) behold! they would certainly have made thee (their) friend!
[74] "And had We not given thee strength thou wouldst nearly have inclined to them a little" (Al-Isaraa 17: 73-74).

Therefore, the Prophet corrected his recitation and read the verses of Surah An-Najm as follows:

[19] Have ye seen Lat, and 'Uzza,
[20] And another, the Third (goddess), Manat?
[21] What! for you the male sex, and for Him, the female?
[22] Behold, such would be indeed a division most unfair! (An-Najm 53: 19-22).

Al-Qimni explains in more detail the reaction of Muslims and non-Muslims to those verses, which were known also as the verses of the Gharaniq[32]. However, more important is that there are verses in the Qur'an, which were changed and replaced by other verses and some that were totally lost. The Qur'an itself testifies to this fact in the following verses:

"When We substitute one revelation for another, - and Allah knows best what He reveals (in stages), - they say, "Thou art but a forger": but most of them understand not" (Al-Nahl 16: 101).

"None of our revelations do We abrogate or cause to be forgotten, but We substitute something better or similar: knowest thou not that Allah hath power over all things?" Al-Baqarah 2: 106).

"Allah doth blot out or confirm what He pleaseth: with Him is the Mother of the Book" (Ar-Ra'd 13: 39).

Therefore, the verses of the Gharaniq or the so-called satanic verses were attributed to the desire of the Prophet and the deception of Satan.

"Never did We send a Messenger or a prophet before thee, but, when he framed a desire, Satan threw some (vanity) into his desire: but Allah will cancel anything (vain) that Satan throws in, and Allah will confirm (and establish) His Signs: for Allah is full of knowledge and wisdom" (Al-Hajj 22: 52).

The story of the Gharaniq, and some verses in the Qur'an, which seemed to contradict each other led early Muslim scholars to establish what was known as the Nasikh (abrogating) and Mansukh (abrogated). There are three kinds of Nasikh and Mansukh in the Qur'an: -

1- The legal power of a verse is abrogated but its recitation remains.

2- The recitation of a verse is abrogated but its legal power remains.

3- The legal power and recitation of a verse both are abrogated. (Ibid: 570).

(I) The legal power of a verse is abrogated but its recitation remains: The famous examples of this type of abrogation are the verses of Stoning and of the Breastfeeding of an adult. Most of the Muslim scholars agreed that the verse of stoning was revealed to the Prophet and later on taken up to heaven. It was said that the caliph "Umar Ibn al-Khattab said "we used to read the verse which said if Al-Sheikh *or "old man"* and Al-Sheikha *or "old woman"* commit adultery stone them completely for the pleasure they had obtained… and if I do not hate that the people would say "Umar had added to the Qur'an I would have added it" (Ibid: 573). However the verses of the Qur'an, which talk about adultery, do not say to stone the adulterer or the adulteress.

"If any of your women are guilty of lewdness, take the evidence of four (reliable) witnesses from amongst you against them; and if they testify, confine them to houses until death do claim them, or Allah ordain for them some (other) way" (An-Nisa 4:15).

"The woman and the man guilty of adultery or fornication flog each of them with a hundred stripes: let not compassion move you in their case, in a matter prescribed by Allah, if ye believe in Allah and the Last Day: and let a party of the Believers witness their punishment" (Al-Nur 24:2).

Nevertheless, the Shari'a laid down the stoning punishment for the married man/woman if they commit adultery because of the saying of the caliph "Umar.

The verse about breastfeeding of an adult was based on a report by "A'isha in which she said "the verse of stoning and the verse of breastfeeding of an adult were revealed to the Prophet, and when he fell sick we became busy about his sickness. A tame animal ate the scroll that contained the verses. The Prophet died and the verses used to be read as part of the Qur'an" (Ibid 580). The question that Al-Qimni found difficult to answer was "whether the verse of breastfeeding of an adult was abrogated before the tame animal ate it, or whether it had been considered an abrogated verse because it was not found among the copies of the Qur'an which were collected by the third Caliph Uthman Ibn 'Affan because the animal ate it?" (Ibid: 581). The story of the breastfeeding was narrated in a Hadith by "A'isha in which she says,

"One day Sahla Bint Sohil came to the Prophet and said to him: I saw in the face of Abi Huzifa (her husband, that means she saw him angry) whenever Salem came to our house. The Prophet said to her: breastfeed him. She said, how can I breastfeed him and he is a grown up man? He said; do I not know he is a grown up man? Then she came later on and said; I swear by Allah O Prophet of Allah I do not see anything on the face of Abi Huzifa that I hate" (Ibid: 580).

Following the advice of the Prophet to Sahla Bint Sohil, "that "A'isha used to order her sister Um Kalthum and the daughters of her brother to breastfeed anyone from men whom they wanted to enter to them" (Ibid). The question: how can a grown up woman or girl breastfeed a grown up man? Would not that make the man to be sexually aroused? And what about the woman? Would she remain calm when a grown up man's lips touch the nibble of her breast? According to Al-Qimni the verse of breastfeeding of an adult should be treated the same as the verse of the stoning of al-Sheikh and al-Sheikhah (old man and old woman) if they commit adultery. However, the Muslim scholars, for no clear reason, retained the legal punishment of stoning and not the legal right for Muslim women to breastfeed the men whom they love to have visit their houses. The breastfeeding of an adult continued until the death of the Prophet as ʿAʾisha practiced it and recommended her sister and nieces to do so. Some Muslim scholars argue that the verse of breastfeeding was abrogated. But the question of al-Qimni remains as when, how, and by whom the verse was abrogated? Al-Qimni rejects this argument because no abrogation could be accepted after the death of the Prophet. This is a generally accepted principle. Once again someone might wonder, how the young, pretty, and beloved wife of Muhammad, ʿAisha used to breastfeed the young men whom she wanted them to enter her house? By the way, when Muhammad died ʿAisha was eighteen years old and that means she was still young and sexually active?

(II) **The recitation of a verse is abrogated but its legal power remains:** Some of the Muslim Muhajireen (immigrants who came with the Prophet from Makka to Medina) used to address the Prophet by his name and visit him without any invitation or information. This improper behaviour irritated the Prophet and hence the Qurʾan found a good solution for it (Ibid: 583). It prescribed certain a mount of money to be paid to the Prophet by any one who wanted to meet and talk to him (Ibid). Al-Qimni interpreted the word Sadaqa (charity) to mean consultation fees to be given to the Prophet, but the word could mean also giving charity or alms to the poor people.

"O ye who believe! when ye consult the Messenger in private, spend something in charity before your private consultation. That will be best for you, and most conducive to purity (of conduct). But if ye find not (the wherewithal), Allah is Oft-Forgiving, Most Merciful" (Al-Mujadila 58:12).

This verse led many Muslims to avoid meeting and consulting the Prophet. When the curious Muslims learned their lesson, God abrogated the above verse and replaced it with the following verse,

"Is it that ye are afraid of spending sums in charity before your private consultation (with him)? If, then, ye do not so, and Allah forgives you, then (at least) establish regular prayer; practise regular charity; and obey Allah and His Messenger. And Allah is well-acquainted with all that ye do" (Al-Mujadila58: 13).

The verse of the Sword was another example of a verse that abrogated other verses.

[5] But when the forbidden months are past, then fight and slay the Pagans wherever ye find them, and seize them, beleaguer them, and lie in wait for them in every stratagem (of war); but if they repent, and establish regular prayers and practise regular charity, then open the way for them: for Allah is Oft-Forgiving, Most Merciful (At-Touba 9: 5).

According to Ibn Al-Arabi "everything in the Qur'an which speaks about forgiveness for unbelievers and avoiding killing them have been abrogated by the verse of the sword... this verse has abrogated a hundred and twenty-four verses" (Ibid: 584). The problem began when Uthman collected the verses of the Qur'an and arranged them in a way that the abrogated verses were mixed up with the abrogating verses (Ibid). This arrangement led to the appearance of discrepancies and contradiction in the 'Uthmanic Qur'an, which is used until our present day.

(III) The legal power and recitation of a verse both are abrogated:

According to "A'isha', the Surah of Al-Ahzab was two hundred verses when the Prophet was still alive, but 'Uthman collected only seventy or seventy-one verses of it (Ibid: 590). And Muslama Ibn Mukhlid said "tell me of two verses which were not written in the Qur'an and when no one was able to tell him he recited 'those who believe, immigrate, and fight for the cause of Allah by their money and souls; behold they were the successful. And those who gave him shelter, victory, and contested against the people upon whom the wrath of Allah remained, to them no soul knows what has been stored for them as a reward for what they had done" (Ibid: 591).

In order to prove that the present Qur'an is not complete, Al-Qimni referred to the case of "Aisha' in which she instructed the writer of her Qur'an to add the verse "Keep the prayers and the middle prayer and the prayer of Al-'Asir and pray to Allah at night" (Ibid). Taha Husyan said in this regard "the Qur'an was revealed in seven letters only[33], and 'Uthman restricted what he would like to restrict from the Qur'an, and burned what he burned from the Qur'an. Accordingly, "Uthman restricted verses that Allah had revealed and burned copies of the Qur'an that contained verses that Muslims learned from the Prophet. It was not right for the Imam Uthman to conceal one verse from the Qur'an or remove verses from it" (Ibid).

According to Al-Qimni, the presence of Nasikh and Mansukh verses in the Qur'an should not be understood as contradiction. For him the book of Allah is perfect, complete, and free from any contradiction. However, it is difficult for a serious researcher not to see some contradictions in the Qur'an. For instance, when the Prophet immigrated to Medina "necessity and wisdom required that some verses of the Qur'an should go before the Muslims to praise the children of Israel, their prophets, and the admission that Allah has preferred them to other nations, that in their Torah there was guidance and light, and they should follow what it is written in their Torah" (Ibid: 588). However, this friendly atmosphere towards the Jews had changed for no other reason except that their alliance was not needed "after the victory of the Great Badr in which Muslims possessed weapons and great wealth and strength" (Ibid: 589).

It is surprising that after Badr the Prophet suddenly discovered that the Jews "had corrupted the original Torah and hence it became necessary to kill them for changing the verses of Allah" (Ibid). Al-Qimni saw the same behaviour of the Qur'an towards the Christians "after the need for Abyssinia and its Nagashi was over, the revelation must say its word towards the Christian dogmas" (Ibid). When the Muslims were small in number and in a state of weakness in Makka "the wise verses of the Qur'an suited their weakness among the hostile majority, and therefore the verses granted freedom of faith and that there is no compulsion in religion and that the judgment should be left to Allah on the Day of Resurrection" (Ibid). Al-Qimni continues "after the immigration from Makka to Medina, and after the Great Badr and the changing from the state of weakness to the state of power, came the Nasikh verses to abrogate the freedom of faith and command Muslims to fight and kill non-Muslims" (Ibid). Therefore, al-Qimni resolves the seeming contradictions in the Qur'an by placing the various verses into the historical context of their revelation or "asbab al-nuzul".

Chapter 7 Endnotes

[31] Writings in italic and the translation are mine.

[32] Gharaniq in Arabic means "high birds" but here most probably means intercessors or goddesses. The Makkan Arabs believed that these three goddesses-Lat, 'Uzza, and Manat- are the daughters of Allah (The Creator) and hence their idols were revered and worshipped in Makka.

[33] In this context, Al-Qimni referring to Taha Husyan's book, *Fi al-Shi'ir al-Jahili (Pre-Islamic Poetry)* published in 1926. Husyan excludes the Arabic letters that contain dots because Abu Al-Aswad Al-Dwali was the first scholar to add dots to the letters of the Qur'an, Sabawai added punctuation to the verses of the Qur'ann, and Al-Nabiqa Al-Zibiani put the rules of the Arabic grammar.

Chapter Eight

SAYYID AL-QIMNI

Sayyid Mahmoud al-Qimni is a "progressive writer and Cairo University lecturer on sociology of religion" (The Middle East Media Research Institute, September 27, 2004: 1). Al-Qimni was born on March 13, 1947 in the city of Al-Wasita, which is located in the Southern province of Egypt (Abd al-Gadir Feb 2, 2004). His father, Sheikh Mahmoud al-Qimni graduated from Al-Azhar University. Sheikh al-Qimni was a very religious traditionalist Azharite and always dressed in a traditional way. In his large house, Sheikh al-Qimni organized religious gatherings to substitute for his days in Al-Azhar. Most of those gatherings took place during the month of Ramadan. Although Sheikh al-Qimni was a very religious man he was also open to other people's opinions. Accordingly, he adopted the ideas of the Egyptian reformist Muhammad Abduh.

His son Sayyid was brought up in this religious home. He was sick from childhood. The sickness was a heart problem (Mahmoud 2004: 1); al-Qimni stated in his interview with Asharif Abd Al-Gadir (2004) that his childhood was not happy because of this early sickness. Despite this, he graduated from A'in Shams University, Cairo from the faculty of philosophy. After studying philosophy al-Qimni joined al-Azhar University and studied Islamic history. The defeat of Egypt by Israel in 1967 was a turning point in his life. He wanted to find the reason for the defeat and this led him to concentrate his life on studying Islam and other religions. He undertook thorough research on Islamic sciences such as fiqh, philosophy, and kalam in different schools of thought, but did not decide to be a writer until 1985. His writings were concentrated on the critical study of Islam and Islamic discourse. However, the occupation of Kuwait by Sadam's troops in 1991 changed the attitude of al-Qimni from being a Nasarite who believed in a single Arabic community to one who focused on the Egyptian community. In other words, Egypt as a nation replaced Egypt as an Arab country in his thought. At this junction, liberalism became a belief and dogma for al-Qimni. Although al-Qimni did not mention it explicitly, from the interview with Asharif Al-Abd Al-Gadir and his early writings one could deduce that Al-Qimni was working in Kuwait at the time Sadam's invasion took place. Many Arabs had to flee Kuwait leaving behind their properties and money.

Al-Qimni was concerned to understand the cause of Egypt's 'backwardness'. About this he said, "what disturbs me most is the backwardness of my nation and its civilized defeat. Every project I take is meant to discover some unknown cause for the reason of Egypt being behind other civilized nations" (Abd Al-Gadir, Feb, 2004: 4). At the same time, he wanted to re-write the Prophet's Sira or "Biography" in accordance to its historical development, which led to the foundation of a political Islamic state at the time of Muhammad. He discusses this in his volume, *al-Islamiat (The Islamisms)*, which contains his two controversial books, *Al-Hizb Al-Hashmi Wa Tasis Al-Dawla Al-Islamyia (The Hashmite Party and The Foundation of the Islamic State)*, and *Hurub Dawlat al-Rasul (The Wars of the Prophet's State)*. In his books *Al-Ustora Wa Al-Turath (The Myth and the Heritage)* and *Kisat Al-Khlik (The Story of Creation)*, al-Qimni traces the origins and roots of myths and how they found their way into Judaism, Christianity, and Islam.

One of the main projects which al-Qimni is currently undertaking is the re-organization of the Qur'an in a chronological order. According to al-Qimni, the present Qur'an was arranged by caliph Uthman like walls (Arabic Surs from which comes the word Surah, used to designate chapters of the Qur'an), starting from the longest Surahs to the shortest ones. Due to this arrangement the Nasikh or "abrogating" verses became near the Mansukh or "abrogated" verses, a second law before a first law, the verse of peace near the verse of war, and the verses of freedom of faith mixed with the verses which made Islam compulsory with no other faith accepted. Therefore, the ordinary Muslim cannot understand the Qur'an without a Mufassir or "an interpreter" (and a Mufti). Al-Qimni believes that this was a key reason for the monopolization of the Qur'an by a group of scholars who claim that their interpretation is the only right one. Any other interpretation is considered Kufr or "unbelief". In his interview with Abd al-Gadir, al-Qimni expressed his views as follows:

1- The Qur'an needs to be re-arranged and looked upon more carefully.

2- There is no priesthood in Islam.

3- The law of apostasy does not exist in the Qur'an.

4- Muslim scholars want to both recognize woman's rights and at the same time label her as deficient in religion and intellect, which is a contradiction.

5- The concept of Jihad is a communal and racist idea and is rejected by the modern time.

6- What the early Muslim Mujahidun or "fighters" did in those countries they invaded needs to be apologized for today (Abd al-Gadir 2004: 4).

Al-Qimni controversially argues that the occupation of Egypt by Arabs should be counted as the longest foreign occupation in the world (al-Muhsin, Feb 26, 2004: 1). The backwardness of Egypt came, he believes, from the acceptance of this Arabic occupation and the adoption of the Arabic culture. Al-Qimni's view undoubtedly stirred discontent amongst the moderate and the radical Muslim thinkers in Egypt. In his book, *Al-Fashoon wa al-Watan (Fascists and the Nation)*, al-Qimni states his views about the effect of Arabic culture on Egypt in the following words:

There are three cultures in Egypt, and no one of them should be exalted above the other two. These cultures are the ancient Egyptian culture, the Coptic culture, which is written in Greek letters, and the Arabic Islamic culture, which came from Arabia. By making the Arabic culture to rule over other cultures one goes against the principle of Egyptian nationality. Any one who calls for the reign of the Arabic culture in Egypt does not see in other cultures a culture for himself, and that means he does not think as an Egyptian, but as an Arab invader. Therefore, we repeat, the logic of communalism is always followed by a cancellation of the concept of the nation and worse than that it destroys this nation itself (al-Qimni 1999: 49).

Accordingly, al-Qimni argues that "the identity of the Egyptian Muslim should be Egyptian and not Afghani or Hijazi, and the identity of the Egyptian Christian should be Egyptian and not American or French" (Ibid). When Egyptian identity is based on the Arabic and Islamic alliance, then "the Muslim will feel more related to the Bosnian Muslim than the Coptic Egyptian. Therefore, shedding the blood of the Coptic Egyptian becomes halal or "permissible," and he must pay the price for what is happening in Bosnia and Hursik" (Ibid: 51).

Referring to a speech delivered by al-Qimni at the International Book Exhibition in Cairo on Jan 14, 2004, the Muslim Brothers newspaper "al-Akhwan al-Muslimun" argued that the speech was meant to demolish all the pillars of Islam ("al-Akhwan al-Muslimoon,"

Jan 1, 2004: 1). The newspaper stated further that al-Qimni had said the first Muslim invaders had stolen all the treasures of Egypt and therefore Egypt should not be called an Arab and Muslim country any more. Islam should not be the official religion of Egypt and the Shari'a laws should not be considered the main basis for the Egyptian constitution. In an article entitled "Doubtful Books," in al-Watan newspaper, Abd Allah al-Samti said "writers like Khalil Abd al-Karim, Sa'id al-Ashmawi, Sayyid al-Qimni, al-Sadiq Nihum, and Nawal al-Sa'adawi want people to believe that the Qur'an is not revealed but the word of Muhammad" (al-Samti, March 15, 2002: 1). For these writers Muhammad was just a great man and not the seal of the prophets (Ibid). In another interview conducted by Hala Mahmoud for "Middle East Times," the interviewer stated;

Sayyid Al Qimni deals with early Islamic history like no other Egyptian historian will dare. He saves himself from being labeled either an apostate or a tool of the West by only using sources approved by Al Azhar, but many of his conclusions would make Nasr Hamid Abu Zayd blanch. Works such as *Al Hizb Al Hashimi (The Hashemite Faction), Al Dawla Al Mohamadiya (The Mohammedite State),* and *Hurub Dawlat Al Rasul (The Wars of the Prophetic State),* trace the tenets of Islam to political pressures rather than revelation, while books like *Al Nabi Ibrahim (The Prophet Abraham)* find a secular explanation for the myths of the earliest Prophets (Mahmoud, Middle East Times, p. 1)

When Hala Mahmoud asked al-Qimni whether he faced any physical or verbal attack by the radical Islamists, he replied;

Ideologically and physically. First there was Fahmi Howiedy in Al Ahram. He said I am more of a risk than Salman Rushdie in an article entitled 'Pluralism without going beyond the bounds' in March 1989. He wrote, 'They differ from [Rushdie's] books in the degree of the insult, but not in the essence'; 'it damages what is sacred'; and 'we must stop this writing.' He only referred to me as SQ but he mentioned my books by name. Four years ago, in Al Islam Watan (Islam is a Nation), a general in the Interior Ministry, Essam Eddin Abdel Azayem wrote, 'Oh Lord, please do not allow anyone like this man into our land. They destroy our religion and give birth to unbelievers.' Dr. Muhammad Ahmed Al Musayyar, in Al Nour of July and August 1992, wrote 'Someone shut this voice up.' In 1989, after the Howeidy article, I was driving in [the Giza village] of Badrshein when someone shot at me with a Kalashnikov. I had kids with me. It was a warning. If they wanted to kill me, they could have (Ibid: 11).

Al-Qimni was counted by Samir Sarahan as one of the most provocative thinkers in Egypt due to his "written revisionist histories of the era of the Prophet" (Sarahan Feb 5, 1998: 1). In a long debate on Al-Jazeera Radio with Kamal Habib, a radical Islamist, Al-Qimni said that "we are at the bottom of the sea of darkness because we teach our children at school only Islamic religion and Arabic language" (Ibid: 15). In other words, the education system in Egypt and other

Arab countries produces people who only know how to pray and speak Arabic. Besides that, Al-Qimni believed the educational curriculum in Muslim countries produces terrorists (Ibid: 11).

According to Sayyid Mahmoud Al-Qimni, the religious authority in Egypt condemns any Muslim man/woman as an apostate, deserving to be killed for committing one of the following offences, (here al-Qimni is referring to a modern list prepared by an Azharite scholar, known as Sheik Sabiq):

1- Permitting the forbidden and forbidding the permissible.

2- **Declaring unbelief, atheism, and claiming to have received a revelation from God.**

3- Insulting the Prophet or the religion.

4- **Attacking the book of the Qur'an and the Sunna.**

5- Throwing the books of the Hadith or the Fiqh in the garbage cans and spitting on them.

6- Denying the possibility of seeing Allah on the Resurrection Day.

7- Denying the possibility of suffering in the grave and the questioning of Munkir and Nakir (he did not mention with them Al-Su'aban Al-Aqr'a or "the bald-headed Snake" even though it is one of the necessary articles of the faith).

8- Denying the Sorat[34] and the judgment.

9- **Declaring lack of trust on the narrators of the Hadith.**

10- **Declaring trust on the narrators of the Hadith, but doubting the formation of a specific hadith.**

11- **Telling the Muslim an interpretation or an opinion that he has not heard about it before.**

12- **Leaving the laws of the Book and the Sunna and preferring human-made laws**.

(Al-Qimni 2004: 235, emphasis is mine).

Rab Al-Zaman (The Lord of This Time) and the Court Case

In August 18, 1997, based on a report by the Islamic Research Academy of Al-Azhar University (IRA) "the state security stormed print houses to confiscate the novel <u>Rab Al-Zaman ("God of Times")</u> by Sayyid Al-Qimni" (Engel 1998: 1). Due to an Emergency Law issued in 1981 after the assassination of Sadat "the prosecutors at the state security are empowered to confiscate materials before a court decision" (Ibid: 3). However, in order to make the matter more legal, the prosecutors referred the author of the book in question to the North Cairo Court of First Instance. The Court met on September 15, 1997, "under the chairmanship of Mr. Salama Selim" ("Legal Research and Resource Center for Human Rights" 1998: 1). The report further stated:

One book written by Islamist thinker Sayyid Al Qimni was seized by police on August 16 without a court order, after officials at the Islamic Research Center at Al Azhar ruled that it should be banned for violating religious laws and norms. On September 15, a court ruled in favor of lifting the confiscation and releasing all copies of the book, *The God of Times* (Ibid).

The Legal Research and Resource Center for Human Rights "represented Al-Qimni in Court" (Ibid).

The prosecutors for the state security requested that the court ban the book "on the basis of Article 198 of the Penal Code for the propagation and the prejudice – in writings – of ideas resenting heavenly religion, and on the basis of the report by the annexed Islamic Research Academy" (Ibid). Commenting on the book and trial, Andrew Hammond said:

> His book is little more than a collection of articles published over the last few years in Egyptian newspapers. He is accused of "deriding the religions…His tormentors he has debated face to face on satellite television. Yet a special committee of Al Azhar institution that comes closest to orthodoxy in Sunni Islam has chosen Sayyid Al- Qimni's *Rabb Al Zaman (God of Times) as the banner book in a campaign to ban 196 books that they say represent an iconoclastic secular lobby that is growing alarmingly in confidence (Hammond 1997: 1).*

CHARGES AGAINST THE BOOK The Islamic Research Academy of Al-Azhar University mentioned the following charges against the book:

1- The book included sarcasm and derision of Islamic 'ulama's [scholars], and the nation 'the best ever sent to people'.

2- It refers to page 32, based on what the Torah says about Abraham, his sons Ishmael and Isaac and his son Jacob, and his grandchildren. It also cited other statements from page 32- page 41 and compared it to narrative *(of Torah)*.

3- It also cited page 66 of the book, which claims that it is the Pharaohs who built the Ka'ba.

4- It also referred to page 67, which says that the Prophets visited Egypt and learnt monotheism from it and preached it in their own countries when returned.

5- On page 80 the author reports the story of Zenoubia (Queen of Tadmor) and Satan thereby discrediting Prophet Solomon's rule.

6- On page 84 he said that god Merdouk, one of the idols worshipped in Iraq at the time of Abraham, was one of those destroyed by Abraham, this needs to be proved by extensive research.

7- He mentioned on pages 107 and 109 several incidents he attributed to Caliph Uthman Ibn 'Affan which do not befit him.

8- On pages 111, 112, and 115 he said words discrediting two leading Muslim scholars namely Mohammed al-Ghazali and Abu Azayem.

9- On pages 141-149 he discredited Sheikh Abdel Sabour Shahin. On pages 147 and 148 he referred to the case of Dr.

Nasr Abu Zayd and Sheikh Shahin's attitude towards Abu Zayd. On page 151 he derided the jurisdiction.

10- On page 154 he said 'Umar Ibn al-Khattab had prohibited what had been permissible with regard to women and pilgrimage" (Ibid: 1-2).

11- The report stated the book shows contempt for the prophet Yusuf (*Joseph)* and for the Caliph Uthman Ibn Affan. (Warr 1997: 2).

The caution that Al-Qimni exercised in writing his book, <u>Al-Hizb Al-Hashimi (The Hashimite Faction)</u>, was not enough to protect him from the attack of the Islamic Research Academy of Al-Azhar University in his book, <u>Rab Al-Zaman (The Lord of Time)</u>. In his former book, Al-Qimni used sources approved by Al-Azhar University and therefore the "ulama" or "scholars" could not find substantial evidence to ban the book. However, in his later book, Al-Qimni not only criticized the Azhar's scholars, but his criticisms extended to the Hadiths of the Prophet Mohammad and the holy Qur'an.

The Decision of the Court: The decision of the court was most probably based on the arguments Al-Qimni presented to refute the allegations against the book. This understanding could be deduced from the opinions of the readers who read the book and the court file. So far I have not obtained the court file, but I will try to get it and then I will be able to see how Al-Qimni succeeded in refuting the charges against his book. In fact I have received an e-mail from the publisher, which stated that the book, the court file, and the media coverage have been mailed to me by May 23, 2004. However, I will give a summary of the Judge's decision on the book, which had been stated briefly in the report of the Legal Research and Resource Center for Human Rights, which represented Al-Qimni in Court.

As regarding the charges against the way the book presented the Hebrew Prophets Abraham, Ishmael, Isaac, and Joseph in pages 32-42 the judge said "the author's basing his criticism of a film directed by Yusuf Shahin and his using the Torah's language to respond to what he considers a distortion of the Torah in the film as well as his addition to the titles and situations referred to in the Torah is not a scientific approach to the study of the Torah as the author claims" ("Legal Research and Resource Center for Human Rights" 1998: 2). I will quote a few passages from the book to show how Al-Qimni spoke about the Hebrew ancestors and the film of Yusuf Shahin Al-Muhagir, (The Immigrant). According to Al-Qimni, Yusif Shahin was not honest in his film because he tried to hide the fact that the movie was about the story of Joseph as mentioned in the Torah and not the Qur'an. "The film producer" said Al-Qimni "put a poster in front of his film in Arabic language stating that the movie has nothing to do with Prophet Yusuf (*Joseph*) and at the same time another poster in French language stating this story is the story of the Patriarch Joseph" (Ibid: 32). One more serious mistake the producer made was that he "confused the story of Joseph and the story of Moses in his film (Ibid: 35). When the hero of the film, the Immigrant entered Egypt the film narrated the story of Joseph and when he left Egypt that of Moses. As regarding the Jews' claim to prophecy and the Promise Land, Al-Qimni stated:

They were a holy nation that God preferred to other nations, they were a series of intelligent and sanctified prophets, their father was a prophet and begot a prophet, in a series of inheriting prophecy as they inherited the land of Palestine, the best descendent from the best descendent, in holiness they were superior to other misguided nations, their far grandfather was Abraham the friend of God, and their fathers were Isaac, and Jacob who was nicknamed Israel, and his children were the honored patriarchs, and from them came the beautiful youth and tempting Joseph who became the minister of all the treasures of Egypt… and after him came Moses the greatest prophet of Israel…then King David and his son King Solomon, and this last King established a great kingdom for which the religious books and legendary books gave songs and praises, he had authority over the beasts, Al-Hoam, Jinn, and Al-Afariat (*demons*), and in his time Israel became the richest country until silver filled the streets like sand (according to Torah[35]) and in the Islamic heritage he became one of the four kings in the world who ruled from one end to the other end of the earth (Ibid: 37-38).

On page 41 Al-Qimni said, "in fact, if we measure the great establishments of the third Tatmosis or the second Remises or Nebuchadnezzar, the establishments of Solomon became very insignificant in comparison". In regard to this account, the judge concluded "in scientific research there is no infringement on the sanctity of prophets so long as there is no addition to what the Torah says … this is a totally safe and sound approach and does not infringe upon Islam" ("Legal Research and Resource Center for Human Rights" 1998: 2).

The court also cleared Al-Qimni from the allegation that he said things, which were not appropriate about the caliph Uthman Ibn Affan. According to the judge what the author stated about Uthman was quoted from well-known and reliable Islamic religious sources such as:

1- Al Bedaya wal nehaya (The Beginning and the End) by Sheikh Emad Ibn al-Nedaa Ishmael Ibn Omar Ibn Kathir. See pp. 190 and 251 of section 7, vol. 4 of al-Ghad al-Arabi edition.

2- Al Tabakat al Kobra by Mohammed Bin Sa'ad, verified by professors Hamza al Nasharti, Abdel Hafiz Faraghali and Abdel Hamid Mustafa. See page 623, vol. 11 Al Ahram distributions.

3- Tarikh al Islam al Zahabi (The Golden Age of Islam), vol. 11 page 123 and subsequent pages (published by al-Ghad al Arabi).

4- Zoamaa al Islam (Leaders of Islam) by Dr. Hassan Ibrahim, published by the Egyptian Book Organization, Religious Works, 1997 edition, p. 401 and subsequent pages" (Ibid: 3-4).

What Al-Qimni had said about Sheikh Mohammed Al-Ghazali and the general Essam Eddin Abul Azaym, the judge said "though strongly worded, we see it as permissible criticism in debates between leading scholars, jurisprudents and thinkers, and common in the history of intellectual criticism and debates" (Ibid: 4). Moreover, what the author said about Sheikh Abd Sabour Shahin's role in the trial of Nasr Hamid Abu Zayd, the judge ruled "can be seen as a debate between the author's and Shahin's views" (Ibid). In short the judge referred to the rest of the charges and cleared the author from all of them on the ground that none of them would lead to the confiscation of the book. Therefore, the judge concluded his statement by saying that "for all these reasons we have decided to annul the order to seize the book <u>Rab al Zaman wa Derasaat Okhra</u> by its author Mr. Sayyid Mahmoud Al-Qimni, and release the book and everything used for its printing" (Ibid: 5).

Al-Qimni's analysis of the early history of Islam: In most of his writings, al-Qimni is trying to prove that the history of Islam is a forged or falsified history. In order to do so, al-Qimni wrote his three controversial books, *Al-Hizb Al-Hashmi Wa Tasis Al-Dawla Al-Islamyia (The Hashmite Party and The Foundation of the Islamic State), (1989), Hurub Dawlat al-Rasul, (The Wars of the Prophet's State), (1996),* and *Rab Al-Zaman (The Lord of Times), (1996).* His first book, *Al-Hizb Al-Hashmi Wa Tasis Al-Dawla Al-Islamyai,* put him in conflict with the 'ulama' or "scholars" of al-Azhar al-Sharif University. According to Sivan, "in 1989, al-Qimni published his trial-blazing book *Al-Hizb Al-Hashemi*, where he ventured into a hitherto taboo area, the life of the Prophet (he interpreted the Prophet's struggle with Makka in terms of power politics). A leading Islamist spokesman dubbed him 'the Arab Salman Rushdie" (Sivan 2003: 39). In this book, al-Qimni tried to prove that the grandfather of the Prophet Muhammad, Abd al-Mutalab had prepared the way for the foundation of the Islamic State. The implication of this assertion is that the actual founder of the Islamic State was not the prophet, but that the Prophet completed what his grandfather had already begun. Moreover, the book tried to prove that many Islamic doctrines incorporated in the Qur'an were actually borrowed from ideas of the followers of the Hanafyia, Judaism, Sabians, and pagan Arabs' religion. The book also mentioned some poetic verses composed by Arab poets who either lived before Islam or they were contemporary to Muhammad, which were copied directly in the Qur'an and became part of the holy scripture of Islam. Such an assertion could be understood by Muslim scholars as denying the divine origin of the Qur'an and accusing the prophet Muhammad of theft or to put it in today's language, of plagiarism. In this way, the Qur'an becomes a "cultural product" and its "pre-existence in the preserved Tablet" is denied (Najjar 2002: 194). Nevertheless, the Muslim scholars of al-Azhar could not refute al-Qimni because he relied for his historical critique on Islamic sources that have been considered authentic by the 'ulama' themselves. Condemning al-Qimni would mean casting doubt on these Islamic sources, which are collectively agreed upon by all scholars as authentic books. The most important "al-Azhar approved sources" that al-Qimni uses in his writings are the works of al-Tabari, al-Qortobi, al-Suyuti, Ibn Kathir, al-Bihaqi, al-Halabi, Ibn Hisham, and Ibn Sa'ad. Commenting on the controversial writings of Sayyid al-Qimni and (Khalil Abd al-Karim), Salwa Ismail states,

These are "al-Azhar approved sources." This represents a line of defense, allowing the authors to argue that the information they call upon to highlight certain aspects of the Makkan society and of the Medinan community is drawn from trusted sources. The authors, as such, do not question the reliability of their sources, as it is part of their offensive to turn their opponents' weapons against themselves. If al-Azhar finds fault with the material, then it must reevaluate the heritage books, an undertaking, which is precisely what the revisionists want to see, accomplished (Ismail 2004: 114).

In his second controversial book, *Hurub Dawlat al-Rasul, (The Wars of the Prophet's State),* al-Qimni again overstepped the boundary set by the Islamic 'ulama' and ventured into a taboo area that is the political life of the prophet Muhammad. In this work, he no longer is criticizing the history of Islam alone, but the political life of the prophet Muhammad. His analysis of the political life of the prophet shows that the prophet dealt deceptively with the Jews. When he needed them at the time of his weakness, he praised their religion and prophets. When the need for the support of the Jews became unimportant to the newly founded Islamic State, the prophet looked for chances to get rid of them. This portrays the prophet as a cunning politician who did everything to achieve his goals. To put it in a modern language, the prophet followed the principle that, "the end justifies the means". Another example was the prophet's attitude towards the religion of his Makkan ancestors. In the beginning of his preaching, the prophet rejected and condemned the pagan religion of his Arab ancestors. In doing so, he followed a peaceful approach and gave everyone the right to choose or reject his message. At the end of his life, the book shows that the prophet had fully turned back to the pagan religion of his ancestors and incorporated all the pagan rituals in Islam, especially the rituals of the Hajj or "pilgrimage". At this stage the Qur'an denied the freedom of religion, and Islam became the only open choice for the pagan Arabs. The Muslim scholars were able to get around the contradictions in the Qur'an through the doctrine of Nasikh and Mansukh or "abrogation". However, al-Qimni sees that the abrogation doctrine does not solve the problem. A better and honest solution is to consider the various political contexts in which the prophet was working. Through this new reading of the political life of the prophet and the doctrines of Islam, al-Qimni's writings divorced themselves from the traditional interpretations of Islam.

In his third controversial book, *Rab Al-Zaman (The Lord of Times)*, al-Qimni ran in trouble with the Muslim scholars of al-Azhar. They could not tolerate him any longer. They convinced the state to ban the book and bring al-Qimni to trial. Al-Qimni's historical critical method, which saved him the trouble of being condemned as an apostate, was not enough this time to protect him from the attack of the 'ulama' of al-Azhar. By bringing him before judge, the 'ulama' thought that they could condemn him legally and expose him publicly. However, as the outcome of the trial shows, he was able to refute all the charges laid against his book, *Rab al-Zaman*. His main argument was that whatever he wrote was already mentioned in the "al-Azhar approved sources". Once again, al-Qimi's critical historical method saved him, and his writings remain irrefutable.

In his book Rab al-Zaman, al-Qimni tried to prove that the early history of Islam was full of forgeries. He used as example, the wars of apostasy that caliph Abu Bakr waged against some Arab tribes. According to al-Qimni, Abu Bakr's wars were political wars and had nothing to do with religion. He waged his wars against those who refused to accept his claim to lead the Muslim community. In order to justify his wars, Abu Bakr clothed them with divinity. He fabricated hadith to justify the killing of the Muslim Arabs and attributed the hadith to the Prophet. Al-Qimni's main objection is that those wars were forged and taught to the Muslims in schools and religious institutions as just and holy wars. Al-Qimni also criticized the third caliph Uthman Ibn 'Affan as corrupted leader and his assassination by some of the prophet companions came as a result of his bad leadership. In order to justify Uthman, the Muslim historians suppressed the facts and fabricated a story through which they blamed the murder of the third caliph on a Jew!

In his writings, "al-Qimni represent a politics of contestation and subversion of the claims to power and authority of Islamic 'orthodoxy'" (Ismail 2004: 102). The main goal of al-Qimni is to abolish "the founding period as a social and political ideal" (Ibid: 103). However, al-Qimni's writings "are likely to stir the sentiments of Muslims against" him. "The ordinary Muslim would not accept that his/her sacred symbols be put in question" (Ibid: 118). On the intellectual and official levels, al-Azhar 'ulama' or "scholars" reacted for two reasons,

> First, that they are the guardians of the absolute truth. Any challenge to the claims to power and authority made in the name of orthodoxy must be stamped out. Second, as guardians, they are better qualified than the ordinary believer to judge and respond to the challenge. As such, the believer should not be involved in this debate. It is assumed that he/ she will react only at the emotional level, being incapable of reacting at the intellectual level (Ibid).

The response of al-Azhar was submitted in a lawsuit to the North Cairo Lower Court in a report prepared by the Islamic Research Academy, a branch of al-Azhar University. The report states that "the writings contain errors and distortion and are misrepresentation of 'what is known to be true in Islam" (Ibid: 117). However, not being able to prove their charges against the writings, "the judge dismissed the allegations made against al-Qimni by the Academy" and "quitted him of the charges" (Ibid). Having failed to condemn him legally, the 'ulama' condemned al-Qimni publicly and accused him of takfir or "unbelief" charges, and "as a result of the takkfir charges, there were fears that his life was in danger. He subsequently went into hiding for a period of time in 1998. The attackers included Dr. 'Abd al-Mu'ti Bayumi, Dean of the al-Azhar University's Faculty of the Fundamentals of Religion, along with many other leading Azhari scholars" (Ibid: 118).

Al-Qimni Recants his writings: On July 17, 2005, Dr. Sayyid Mahmoud al-Qimni received a letter from al-Qaida, Iraqi branch that led by al-Zarqawi. The letter states that al-Qimni would be killed if he does not renounce his past writings and promise not to write any more.

Praise be to Allah alone, and prayer and peace to the one who has no Prophet after him.

You must know, you wicked-unbeliever who is called Sayyid al-Qimni, that five of the brothers of Tawhid and lions of the Jihad have been selected for your killing. They vowed to Allah, the highly exalted that they would come close to Him by knocking down your head, and be cleansed from their sins by shedding your blood. By doing that they would fulfill the command of the greatest Prophet, the prayers of my Lord and greetings to him, who said, "any one changes his religion should be killed."

You false claimer, we do not joke, believe this or do not believe it, but we will not repeat our threat. It will not help you to inform the Egyptian security-men. They cannot protect you. They might do so for a short time and then leave you a prey to the lions of Islam. And this if they agree to protect you at all. Moreover, no private guards can protect you. Your guards cannot stop a bullet fired from a running car or a terrace of a neighboring house. Besides that no protection can stop a bomb from exploding in your car or any other means of assassination. Remember those whom we sent to the graves although they were more difficult to reach than you. The wise man who learns from the mistakes of others.

In order to clear our conscience and established al-Hugah[36] on you, we give you one week to declare your repentance and renounce all your unbelieving writings. You must publish your recant in the magazine "Rose-al-Yusif" the magazine in which you published all your unbelieving writings.

If you persist, you ignorant and deluded one, in riding on your stubbornness and continue in your apostasy and atheism, and the accursed Satan whispered to you that you can defy the group of Jihad, then know that the swords of the believers would fulfill their duty on you. At present you are a dead person walking among the worshippers. You better search for a hole for yourself because the faithful will hunt you for sure.

This is a warning for you, resurrection is our promise, and at the Owner of the Throne the people would know the good.

Signature: The Group of Jihad, Egypt.

Unfortunately al-Qimni was forced to recant and publish his the so-called repentance in the media. According to a report by Caroline Kim "facing threats to his life, a well known dissident Egyptian writer, Sayyid al-Qimni, on July 16 took the unusual step of recanting his past work and vowing to forego future assignments and appearances in the media" (Kim July 15, 2005). I don't think the Muslim world and Egypt in particular will ever produce another honest, courageous, and genius writer as Dr. Sayyid Mahmoud al-Qimni

Chapter 8 Endnotes

[34] A narrow bridge that Muslim believers shall cross on the Resurrection Day.

[35] Torah for Muslims is the Book revealed to Moses but sometime it refers to the Old Testament.

[36] To prove someone's views are heresy and on this basis to condemn him/her as an apostate from Islam.

Chapter Nine

MUHAMMAD'S TEACHINGS ABOUT WOMEN

According to Daniel Boyarin "religion is clearly for many if not for most cultures one of the primary systems for the construction of gendered roles" (Boyarin 1998: 117). Thus, to understand gendered roles in Muslim societies we need to see what the Islamic religion says about the roles of men and women. Many Muslim Feminists today are critically studying and rewriting the issue of gender in Islam. Most of them argue that Muslim women are oppressed and marginalized in Islam. However, they argue that it is not the teaching of the Qur'an, but the tradition, which put women in a lower status. In order to uplift women and give them equal rights as men, Muslim feminists argue that the misogynistic hadiths (sayings of the Prophet) must be disregarded. They believe that these misogynistic hadiths were the creation of a later generation of Muslim leaders and scholars and hence do not represent the true message of the Qur'an, which gives equal rights to men and women. However, many Muslim scholars reject the feminists' views. The fundamentalists argue that the hadiths are authentic sayings of the Prophet and rejecting them means denying the words of the Prophet Muhammad. Moreover, they believe that it is not possible to understand the Qur'an without the hadiths for the latter explain the former.

Accordingly, in the contemporary Muslim world, the Hadith (the life, sayings, and deeds of the Prophet Muhammad) became a matter of disputation among scholars. In one camp, the feminists, reformists, and modernists call for a distinction between the misogynistic message of Islam, which contradicts the true spirit of the religion, and the egalitarian message of the Qur'an, which represents Islam in its purest form. In the other camp, we find the fundamentalists, traditionalists, and conservatives who accept all the traditions of Islam, which are in turn incorporated in the Shari's Law[37]. Though, in a few cases, members of this second group are prepared to distinguish between authentic and non-authentic traditions, the disputations between these two camps have not yet been settled and, due to outside influences, the gulf between the two becomes wider day-by-day. That said, these academic and scholarly issues have not affected the average Muslim woman. Most Muslims today accept the teachings of Islam which have been passed down from generation to generation and preserved in the Shari'a Law, which in turn draws its authority and validity from the Qur'an and the Hadith.

In this paper I would like to examine critically the views of Muslim feminists and see whether their claims can be established despite the long tradition of Islam in which the Sharia law, which is based on the Qur'an and Hadith, became the governing norms and laws of Muslims. Muslim scholars agree upon the authenticity of two collections of the Hadith viz., Sahih[38] Bukhari and Sahih Muslim. Nevertheless, other collections, such as Mauta Malik, Sunan Abu Daud, and Tirimizi, have also been accepted and used in the formation of the Shari'a. In general, "the Hadith collections are works that record in minute detail what the Prophet said and did. They constitute, along with the Qur'an (the book revealed by God), both the source of law and the standard for distinguishing the true from the false, the permitted from the forbidden – they have shaped Muslim ethics and values" (Mernissi 1993: 1). For the majority of Muslims, "the authenticated Hadith is sacred literature, only second in holiness to the Qur'an" (Strowasser 1992: 1). In comparing the authority of the former to the latter:

> The authentic Hadith is believed to be nothing short of revelation [for the Qur'an says of Muhammad] "he does not speak out of low desires. It is not but inspiration inspired" (Q 53: 3-4). The only difference between the Qur'an and the Hadith is that whereas the former was revealed directly through the angel Gabriel with the very letters that are embodied by Allah, the latter was revealed without letters and words (Haqq & Newton 1996: 1)

The Qur'an strongly endorses the authenticity of the Hadith and leaves Muslim men and women with no preference between the two: "Whenever Allah and the Apostle have decided a matter, it is not for a faithful man or woman to follow a course of their own choice" (Q 33: 36).

In spite of this strong belief in the Hadith, today we find that some Muslim scholars, especially the feminists and the reformists, do not hesitate to question the authenticity of the Hadith. They accept the important place that the Hadith occupies in Islam but they want to distinguish between the authentic and non-authentic tradition of the Prophet. They use the Qur'an as a measuring rod. Any Hadith that contradicts the egalitarian spirit of the Qur'an should be rejected. This argument assumes that the Qur'an does not include a misogynistic message within its pages. One of these scholars is Riffat Hassan who states, "It is a clear teaching of the Qur'an that men and women are equal in the sight of God" (Hassan 2001: 63). That said, the egalitarian message of the Qur'an is a controversial issue as well. Some feminists see contradictions in the Qur'an and they support their views by referring to its teachings of men's superiority, polygamy, divorce, and wife beating (Q 4: 34, 4: 3, 2: 228, 2: 282, 6: 10). The Egyptian feminist Nawal El-Saadawi is one of those feminists who see contradictions in the Qur'an. She notes that, "God says in his Book that He created men and women from the same soul and then in another page, says the opposite, that men are superior to the [sic] women" (Saadawi 2001: 4). Thus, the egalitarian message of the Qur'an is not a settled issue.

Those who preach such a message have to travel a long way before they can win even one convert. For "their quest to formulate Qur'anic-based agendas for a renewed Islamic order, the general Muslim reaction to the questioning of Hadith authenticity remains strongly negative" (Strowasser 1992: 1).

Sample of the Misogynistic Hadiths:

Allah's Apostle once said to a group of women; 'I have not seen any one more deficient in intelligence and religion than you. A cautious, sensible man can be led stray by some of you.' The women asked: 'O Allah's Apostle, what is deficient in our intelligence and religion?' He said: 'Is not the evidence of two women equal to the witness of one man?' They replied in the affirmative. He said: 'This is the deficiency of your intelligence.' ... 'Isn't it true that a woman can neither pray nor fast during her menses?' The women replied in the affirmative. He said: 'This is the deficiency in your religion" (Sahih Bukhari, Hadith No. 301 & 856).

The authenticity of the above hadith is beyond dispute. It is mentioned repeatedly in the most authentic two collections of Sahih Bukhari and Sahih Muslim. When Bukhari and Muslim both accept a hadith, it is called "mutafagun 'alayihi" which means "agreed upon." Muslim scholars consider this "the highest degree of authenticity" (Haqq & Newton 1996: 3). The Arabic phrase "al-Nisa nagisatan 'aglyan wa din" (women are deficient in intelligence and religion) is on the tip of every Muslim's tongue. This statement is used by scholars as well as lay people to define women. There is a famous proverb in the Arab countries, which says, "If a woman becomes an ax she will not cut a head." This proverb does not only mean that the woman is weak, but she is utterly useless. To turn to further examples:

The woman is like a rib; if you try to straighten her, she will break. So if you want to get benefit from her, do so while she still has some crookedness (Sahih Bukhari, Vol. VII Hadith No. 113).

Women are ungrateful to their husbands and are ungrateful for the favors and the good (charitable) deeds done to them. If you have always been good (benevolent) to one of them and then she sees something in you (not of her liking), she will say, 'I have never received any good from you (Bukhari Vol. 1 hadith No. 28).

*When a woman comes she comes in the form of a devil (*Sahih Muslim, hadith No. 3240).

The Prophet said: 'I have not left any calamity [fitnah] after me more detrimental to men than women. (Bukhari and Muslim agreed upon this Hadith. Bukhari, Vol. VII, hadith No. 33).

O women! Give alms, as I have seen that the majority of the dwellers of Hell-fire were you (women) (Bukhari Vol. 1, Hadith No. 301).

Amongst the inmates of Paradise the women would form the minority (Sahih Muslim, hadith No. 6600.)

Those who entrust their affairs to a woman will never know prosperity (Mernissi 1993: 49).

Fatima Mernissi notes that:

Some Hadiths (prophetic tradition) originated from Kitab[39]
Bukhari, which are told by the teachers hurt me. They state
that the Prophet said: "Dog, donkey and woman would annul
anyone's prayer whenever they pass ahead them, break off
between the praying man and kiblah[40]." I was shocked to
hear that sort of Hadith and never repeat it with the hopes
that silent would wipe away this Hadith out of my mind. I
asked, "How come the Prophet said that sort of Hadith which
hurt me so much... how could the beloved Muhammad hurt
a little girl who is in her growth, attempt to make him as
pillars of her romantic dreams (Mernissi 1991: 82)

Muslim Women and the Tradition: Perhaps the most accurate
accounts in which Muslim women have been placed by the Islamic
heritage can be found in the writings of the Egyptian Muslim liberal
thinker, Sayyid Mahmoud Al-Qimni. In his book, *Rab Al-Zaman
(The Lord of This Time),* under an article entitled "Women In Religious
Heritage and Legends," which he delivered as a lecture to the People's
Progressive Women's Union, Al-Qimni held the Islamic heritage
responsible for degrading Muslim woman (Al-Qimni 96: 219).
According to him, the religious heritage made the woman to believe
"she has been created from a bent rib, deficient in religion and intellect,
her testimony equals half of a man's, her inheritance is half of a man's,
she cannot divorce" (Ibid: 220). The Muslim woman believes herself
to be a Satan and therefore she cannot control her sexual desires (Ibid:
221). According to the Islamic heritage "woman succumbs to her lust

and not intellect, she has a natural tendency to cheat on her husband, because she was one of the four that could not be trusted, 'money, Sultan, time, and woman" (Ibid: 220). Woman had been created for the comfort and enjoyment of her husband. In that way, the religious heritage made the Muslim woman "to believe herself to be a mere **vagina** and hence she became horma (taboo) and haram (forbidden)" (Ibid: 221, emphasis in the original). Therefore, "if she kept her faith and her vagina and gave enjoyment to her husband and master, she would enter heaven" (Ibid: 220). Woman's faith "could not be perfect except by her complete obedience and submission to her husband and such obedience would secure to her a place in heaven as a prostitute among the many harem of the man" (Ibid: 221). This gloomy picture that Al-Qimni depicted for the Muslim woman irritated many Muslim female professors and ulama or "scholars" of Al-Azhar who believed that Islam had honored the woman and put her in the best place.

Al-Qimni states that the Qur'an gives two contradictory rights for women (Al-Qimni 2004: 170). While some verses make woman equals to man such as in Surahs al-Imran: 195, al-Nahil: 97, al-Touba: 71, al-Ahzab: 35, and al-Maida: 38. This positive attitude towards woman was distorted by Surah al-Nisa 4: 34. In a hadith mentioned by al-Bukhari, the Prophet said, "any people make woman their leader will not prosper" (Ibid). Al-Qimni quotes many verses and hadiths to show that woman has been placed in a low position by Islam.

In this regard, Al-Qimni refers to an incident in which he was condemned as a kafir or "unbeliever" by the female professors and doctors of Al-Azhar University because he exposed in his book, *Al-Fashoon wa Al-Watan, (Fascists and the Nation),* the low status in which Islam put the woman- that she was inferior to man in every respect and made for his sexual pleasure. The main reason for their protest was that Al-Qimni "makes mistake by demanding rights for women, which Islam gave to men only" (Ibid: 177).

The samples of the misogynistic hadiths and the accounts of Al-Qimni give an insight into the theory of women in Islam. It is evident that women are understood as causing constant threats to the social order and the religion and as such they need to be brought under control. Quoting the words of Darlene M. Juschka, "If women are understood to carry the darker elements of culture- the chaotic, the sexual, the irrational- then the suppression of these perceived threats is necessary…" (Juschka 2001: 161).

MEN'S SUPERIORTY OVER WOMEN: The Qur'an states that men and women are equal in regards to their religious obligations, rewards and punishment, and oneness of their creation. (Q 3: 195, 4: 1) However, in other verses it teaches that men are superior and one degree above the women. (Q 4: 34, 2: 228.) The Algerian Fadela M'rabat commenting on the Qur'an verse 4:34 says, "what is really being communicated" through this verse "is that God prefers men over women because the latter are inferior." (Smith 1978: 526.) Men are superior to women in knowledge, power, authority and that is because God prefers the former to the latter and men spend out of their means on women. Moreover, women are thought to be deficient in intelligence and religion.

Women are deficient in Gratitude and as Witness: The Qur'an states, "And call in to witness two witnesses, men; or if the two be not men, then one man and two women, such witness as you approve of, that if one woman errs the other will remind her." (Q 2: 282.)

"Women are ungrateful to their husbands and are ungrateful for the favors and the good (charitable) deeds done to them. If you have always been good (benevolent) to one of them and then she sees something in you (not of her liking), she will say, 'I have never received any good from you." (Bukhari Vol. 1 hadith No. 28.)

Woman is 'AWARAH: There is no definition so widely used and accepted among Muslims for defining the woman than she is **"Awarah."** The term Awarah is defined in Encyclopedia of Islam as "the external genitals, especially of the female." (Haqq & Newton 1996: 5.) The word is derived from the noun "nakedness or nudity." So to put it in a simple meaning "woman is naked."

"Ali reported the Prophet saying: 'Women have ten ('awrat). When she gets married the husband covers one, and when she dies the grave covers the ten."(Reported by Tirmizi as an authentic hadith, Vol II Kitab Adab al-Nikah, hadith p. 65).

In another hadith, Tirmizi reported that woman herself is Awarah. *"The woman is 'awrah. When she goes outside (the house), the devil welcomes her "* (Tirmizi Vol II hadith p. 65).

This hadith says that the Woman is always possessed by demons. So she is dangerous to the Society and hence she suppose to be imprisoned inside her house.

The above two hadiths are pertaining to the woman's covering. However, there is disagreement between the founders of the four schools of the Shari'a. While Maliki and Hanbali schools allow the hands and the face to remain uncovered, the Hanbali and Shafi'i considered them to be 'arawah and hence demand the woman to be completely veiled from head to feet. (Haqq & Newton 1996: 5.) Some extreme group like Supporters of the Prophet's Sunna considered even the woman's voice as 'awarah and therefore would not permit her to speak anywhere.

Woman is a crooked Rib: Bukhari and Muslim agreed upon the following hadith:

"The woman is like a rib; if you try to straighten her, she will break. So if you want to get benefit from her, do so while she still has some crookedness." (Sahih Bukhari, Vol. VII Hadith No. 113.)

In Kitab Adab al-Nikah, al-Tirmizi states; *"three [persons] if you esteem them they will dishonour you and if you dishonour them they will esteem you: the woman, the servant, and the Nabatea[41]."* (Tirmizi: p. 51.)

Men's Rights on Women: Islam has ascribed some rights, which men have on their women. The most important of these rights, is total obedience and submission of the women to their husbands.

Obedience: Many hadiths are reported which comment on Qur'an 4:34.

"There are three (persons) whose prayer will not be accepted, nor their virtues be taken above: The runaway slave until he returns back to his master, the woman with whom her husband is dissatisfied, and the drunk until he becomes sober." (Mishkat al-Masabih, English translation, Book I, Hadith No. 74.)

"Whosever female dies while her husband is pleased with her, will enter Paradise." (Mishkat al-Masabih, English translation, Book I, Hadith No. 60.)

"The prophet of Allah said: When a man calls his wife to satisfy his desire, let her come to him though she is occupied at the oven." (Mishkat al-Masabih, English translation, Book I, Hadith No. 61.)

"The messenger of Allah said: Whenever a man calls his wife to his bed and she refuses, and then he passes the night in an angry mood, the angels curse her till she gets up at dawn." (Bukhari, Vol. VII, Hadith No. 121.)

The above hadith is agreed upon: Muslim reported the same hadith but with slight difference *"When a man calls his wife to his bed, and she refuses, the One Who is in the heaven will be angry with her until he [her husband] is pleased with her."* (Haqq & Newton 1996: 7.)

"Had I ordered anybody to prostrate before any one, I would have ordered women to prostrate before their husbands on account of men's rights over the women ordained by Allah." (Mishkat al-

Masabih, English translation, Hadith No. 70. Reported by Abu Dawood, Ahmad, Tirmizi, Ibn Magah, and Ibn Haban.)

WIFE'S BEATING: The Qur'an states; "... Righteous women are therefore obedient. And those you fear may be rebellious (nushuz) admonish them; banish them to their couches, and beat them..." (Q 4: 34.)

The above verse becomes very controversial among modern scholars. Feminists, reformists, and liberal Muslims argue that this verse does not imply that the husband can beat his wife if she becomes rebellious. They try to find different meanings to the word "edrebouhon" and refer the suitable one to the interpretation of the verse. An example for these efforts can be seen in Asma Parls' book, "BELIEVING WOMEN IN ISLAM." However, these efforts became difficult to accept when we refer the verse to the occasion of its revelation. "the above verse was revealed in connection with a woman who complained to Mohammad that her husband slapped her on the face (which was still marked by the slap). At first the Prophet said to her: 'Get even with him', but then added: 'Wait until I think about it.' Later on the above verse was revealed, after which the Prophet said: 'We wanted one thing but Allah wanted another, and what Allah wanted is best.'" (Haqq & Newton 1996: 9.)

Beating of the wife is allowed by the Shari'a in four cases.

(1) When she does not wear fineries though wanted by the husband,

(2) When she is called for sexual intercourse and she refuses without any lawful excuse,

(3) When she is ordered to take a bath [to clean herself] from impurities for prayer and she refuses, and

(4) When she goes out of her house without permission of her husband.

In Sahih Muslim, 'A'isha narrated a long hadith in which she admitted that the Prophet struck her on her chest until it caused pain (Ibid).

"... He (Muhammad b. Qais) then reported that it was 'A'isha who had narrated this: Should I not narrate to you about myself and about the Messenger of Allah (may peace be upon him)? We said: Yes. She said: When it was my turn for Allah's Messenger (may peace be upon him) to spend the night with me, he turned his side, put on his mantle and took off his shoes and placed them near his feet, and spread the corner of his shawl on his bed and then lay down till he thought that I had gone to sleep. He took hold of his mantle slowly and put on the shoes slowly, and opened the door and went out and then closed it lightly. I covered my head, put on my veil and tightened my waist wrapper, and then went out following his steps till he reached Baqi' He stood there and he stood for a long time. He then lifted his hands three times, and then returned and I also returned. He hastened his steps and I also hastened my steps. He ran and I too ran. He came (to the house), and as I lay down in the bed, he (the holy Prophet) entered the (house), and said: Why is it, O

'A'isha, that you are out of breath? I said: There is nothing.
He said: Tell me or the Subtle and the Aware would inform
me. I said: Messenger of Allah, may my father and mother
be ransom for you, and then I told him (the whole story).
He said: Was it the darkness (of your shadow) that I saw in
front of me? I said: Yes. **He struck me on the chest which**
caused me pain, *and then said: Did you think that Allah and*
His Apostle would deal unjustly?" (Sahih Muslim, book 4,
hadith No. 2127.)

The Hadiths, which speak about women, are countless in number.
A few of them show favor to women. Those few hadiths, which speak
well about women, are referring to her as a mother and not as a wife
or daughter.

> *"Abu Hurairah reported that a man came to the Messenger*
> *of Allah (peace be upon him) and asked: "O Messenger of*
> *Allah, who is the person who has the greatest right on me*
> *with regards to kindness and attention?" He replied, "Your*
> *mother." "Then who?" He replied, "Your mother." "Then*
> *who?" He replied, "Your mother." "Then who?" He replied,*
> *"Your father."*
>
> *"Paradise is under the feet of mothers."*

Dr. Suhaib Hasan commenting on the second hadith said:

"The [above] hadith with this wording is da'if[42], but it's meaning is
contained in the hadith of Ibn Majah and al-Nasa'i that a man came

to the Prophet (may Allah bless him and grant him peace) and said, "O Messenger of Allah! I intend to go on a (military) expedition, but I have come to ask your advice." He said, "Is your mother alive?" He said, "Yes." He said, "Then stay with her, for the Garden is under her feet." (Haqq & Newton 1996: 12).

Feminists, reformists, and liberal Muslims very often quote the above two hadiths to support their views that Islam is an egalitarian religion and that misogynistic hadiths were the invention of latter generations. However, these two hadiths advise sons to be kind to their mothers, but neither the husbands to their wives nor fathers to their daughters. Moreover, the two hadiths are not accepted as authentic because neither Bukhari nor Muslim included them in their collections. Only Ibn Majah and al-Nasa'i mention them. These two collectors are hardly quoted by Muslim scholars.

Having the foregoing mentioned verses and hadiths in the main books of Islam 'Qur'an and Hadith' still some scholars claim that the religion is favouring women and gives them equal rights with men. It is hard to believe such a claim. To accept the egalitarian message of Islam and to deny its misogynistic teachings, for me is only a wishful thinking. Such efforts will not benefit those for whom the efforts are done. Muslim women who live in the West are not liberated because of these efforts but the societies in which they live granted them equality with their men. However, Muslim women who live in Muslim societies are still live under the bondage of Muhammad's teachings about women.

Chapter 9 Endnotes

[37] Islamic law as developed historically in the first two hundred years after the Prophet's death.

[38] Authentic.

[39] Book.

[40] "Ka'aba in Makka as it represents the direction of Prayer for Muslims.

[41] Vegetarian.

[42] Unauthentic.

Chapter Ten

MUHAMMAD'S TEACHINGS ABOUT MARRIAGE

After I have spoken in general about women in Islam, I would like to focus on the effects these teachings have exercised on women's lives. I will refer to marriage in general and concentrate on polygamy. For nothing is more criticized in Islam than the practice of polygamy. Critiques pointed out many reasons to show that women in Muslim societies are treated as secondary citizens with no equal rights to men. However, Muslim as well as non-Muslim scholars singled out polygamy as evidence to the oppression of women in Islam. For that reason, in our modern day, scholars are extensively explored the place of woman in Islam and made polygamy the focus of their researches. The practice of polygamy in Muslim societies considerably decreased today mainly due to the financial factors (one man supporting more than one household.) Besides that, some Muslim countries like Tunisia and Turkey outlawed the practice. Other countries such as Egypt put strict conditions on polygamy to discourage people from practicing it. However, the remaining Muslim countries have not yet taken any positive steps towards discouraging polygamous marriage.

Definition of Marriage: Marriage is defined as "a permanent, immediate, and unconditional civil contract (which is not contingent) between two persons of opposite sexes for mutual enjoyment and procreation of children." (Verma 1988: 56) The two concerned persons who sign the marriage contract are not necessarily the husband and wife. According to Shaf'i and Maliki schools, "a woman is utterly incompetent to enter into a marriage contract either herself or for another even though her guardian should authorize her to do so. A father can contract the marriage of his virgin daughter without asking her consent whatever her age." (Verma 1988: 24) However, other schools of law such as Hanafi and Hanbali give woman the right to express her consent. Most of Arab and African Muslim countries follow Shaf'i and Maliki schools whereas countries like Pakistan, India, and Afghanistan accept the Hanafi and Hanbali schools. There are no specific minimum-age limitations in marriage in Islam. This is because the Prophet Muhammad had married Ayisha at the age of six and slept with her at nine. The recent appeal of Muslim writers for laying down rules to restrict the minimum-age requirements can be attributed to the influence of Western culture in Muslim countries. (Lois 1985: 61

Types of Marriage in Islam: There are three types of marriage in Islam: -

1- Monogamous Marriage: A lawful relationship between one man and one woman.

2- Polygamous Marriage: A lawful relationship between one man and more than one women, not to exceed four wives at a time.

3- Muta'a[43] Marriage: A temporary lawful relationship between a man and a woman. This kind of marriage differs from the ordinary marriage because it does not aim at a continuous married life, but the enjoyment in a lawful way. It has been permitted by the Prophet, but abolished by the second caliph, Omar Ibn al-Khattab. Muta'a is unlawful in Sunni Islam, but practiced until today by the Shi'te Islam. In Iran, it is estimated that over 70% of temporary wives became prostitutes. (Woodsmall 1983: 119.)

POLYGAMOUS MARRIAGE

Islam did not invent polygamy but "made it exclusive to man." (Mernissi 1987: 80.) The Moroccan Professor, Fatima Mernissi argued that, polyandry "marriage of one woman to more than one man" was more practiced in Jahilia[44] period than polygamy "marriage of one man to more than one woman." The Prophet concerned about the fate of women, who were divorced, widowed, or unmarried orphans, decided to create a kind of responsibility system in which a man could protect them, not just as a kinsman but also as a husband. (Mernissi 1987: 80.)

Polygamy Before Islam: Ayisha has said: there were four kinds of marriage before Islam. (al-Sabaq 1981: 18.)

1- Marriage of people today: A man proposes to a woman, and then he pays her dowry and marries her.

2- A man says to his wife, when she becomes clean of her menstruation, send for so and so and sleep with him. This kind of marriage is called "al-Istipda'a."[45]

3- Nikah al-Raht: A woman calls a number of men to her house and sleeps with them. When she becomes pregnant, she will call all of them to her house, and then she will tell them that I knew all of you and became pregnant and gave birth to a child. It is your child so and so.

4- The fourth kind of marriage is the one in which many men will sleep with the woman and she will not forbid anyone of them. These are the prostitutes who put flags at their doors as signs of their intention. When she gives birth to a child the people will see whom the child looks alike. The man who matches the child's resemblance is called his father.

It is clear that all these types of marriages don't match polygamy as instituted by Islam. This proves the point of Fatima Mernissi that Islam made polygamy exclusive to man.

Polygamy In Islam

Qur'anic authority, "And if ye fear that ye will not deal fairly of the orphans, marry of the women who seem good to you, two or three or four and if ye fear that ye cannot do justice (to so many) then one (only) or (the captives) that your right hands possess." (Qur'an 3:4.) This verse does not only sanction a Muslim man to marry up to four wives at the same time, but also allows him without condition or limit to have as many number of concubines as he wishes. The verse is revealed after the battle of Uhud in which many men were killed leaving behind them widows and orphans. In Uhud only seventy men were killed. Therefore, the only justification for sanctioning polygamy is to solve the problem of widows and orphans that caused by war. However, later Muslim scholars found other reasons than war to justify the practice of polygamy. According to al-Ghazali, polygamy is necessary because it satisfies human instinct. (Mernissi 1987: 47). For Al-Ghazali, Muslim women have no need to satisfy their human instincts. This kind of argument reveals to us Muslim theory of sexuality, "… for the man burdened with a strong sexual desire and for whom one woman is not enough to guarantee his chastity [chastity for a married person being abstention from zina, [fornication], its recommended that he adds to the first wife, others. The total should not exceed, however, four" (Mernissi 1987: 47).

Commenting on the (Qur'an 2: 233), Mernissi argues that Islam allows the Muslim man to have anal-sex with his wife against her wish. The verse was revealed when an Ansari woman refused to allow her husband to have anal-sex with her. (Mernissi 1993: 145). The woman went to Um Salama (wife of the Prophet and women's representative) and requested her to bring the matter before Muhammad. When Um Salama inquired from the Prophet a verse descended from Heaven, which says, "Your women are a tilt for you (to cultivate) so approach your tilt in any position you wish" (Qur'an 2: 233). This verse gave men the right to choose the sexual position they want and if they desire they are permitted to sodomize their wives against their wishes (Mernissi 1993: 146).

Syd Qutb did not argue like al-Ghazali about the man's chastity, but used woman's barrenness as an excuse for the man to marry another woman. When the woman is barren, the man will be left with two choices: -

1- Either to divorce her and marry another woman to meet his natural desire to have children, or

2- Keeps his wife and marry another one. (Daagir 2002: 24.)

Qutb's argument, which is used by most Muslims today, is weak because it doesn't take into account the barrenness of man. Moreover, if children were the issue, then the Qur'an would have stated that as a condition for marrying other women.

Al-Sabooni believed that, polygamy protects woman from falling into prostitution. He argued that, when Germany was faced with the problem of having more women than men during World War II, it sanctioned polygamy to solve the problem. (Daagir 2002: 24.) This view agrees with the justification of the Qur'an, but again, if the sanctioning of polygamy were conditioned with an urgent problem then there would be no need to practice it after that problem is solved.

Another line of argument, which has been used by many Muslims today, is that, the number of women in the world is more than men. The ratio is 4:1. This problem can be solved only if every man marries four women. This argument has no statistical data to support it. Moreover, the number of Muslim men who have four wives less than those who don't have. Besides that, the financial problems would not allow many men to marry more than one woman.

Another line of argument, which also gained support among Muslims today, is the claim that the period of childbearing in man is longer than that of the woman. The woman cannot bears children after the age of 50, whereas man can have children until the age of 70.

Rashid Radia is the only Muslim scholar, who openly argues that it is the nature of man that one woman cannot satisfy him. Rashid did not tell us why a man needs more than one woman to satisfy him. (Daagir 2002: 25.)

Polygamy in Islam is associated with the belief that women are sources of pleasure and enjoyment for men. History of Islam revealed that women were used by their male partners for the purpose of entertainment. Examples for this are stories of the Arabian Nights, Kitab al-Aghani of Abi al-Faraj al-Asfahani, the women jawari (female pleasure slaves) for the Abbasid caliphs, and the seventy-two houri, (female creatures in Paradise are supposed to be offered as rewards to male believers. They are described in the Qur'an as beautiful, eternally virgin, and eternally loving.) (Mernissi 1988: 71.) The descriptions of the Houri-women in the Qur'an have great effect on the relationship between men and women in Islam. Men look at their wives as inferior to the houris in beauty, loyalty, and pleasure providing.

"Lo! Those [men] who kept their duty will be in place secure amid gardens and water springs, attired in silk and silk embroidery, facing one another. Even so (it will be.) And We shall wed them unto [huris] fair ones with wide, lovely eyes." (Q 44: 51-54.)

"Therein maidens resting their glances, untouched before them by any man or jinn …. Lovely as rubies, beautiful as coral." (Q 55: 56-58.)

"The fair, the beautiful ones [huris]. With large eyeballs, kept close in their pavilions." (Q 55: 72.)

"Surely for the god-fearing awaits a place of security, gardens and vineyards, and maidens of swelling breasts (kawa'eb)[46] like of age, and a cup overflowing." (Q 73: 33.)

"A woman does not give trouble to her husband in this world, but his wife of the pure-eyed ones [huris] does not say to her: 'Do not give him trouble. May Allah destroy you. He is only a passing guest with

you and it is very near that he will soon leave you to come to us."
(Mishakat al-Masabih, book, 1, hadith No. 62.)

"The Prophet was asked: 'Do we have sex in Paradise? He answered: 'Yes, by him who holds my soul in his hand, and it will be done dahman, dahman (that is the intercourse done with such shove and disturbance). And when it is finished she will return pure and virgin again." (Haqq & Newton 1996: 17.)[47]

Every Muslim man is promised seventy-two huris in Paradise and in addition to them he will be given his earthly wives. (ibid: 17.) The question, which disturbs every Muslim scholar is: what is going to be the share of the women who died without being married? The Qur'an and the Hadith are silent in this regard. Such silence may be the reason, which made orthodox scholars to conclude that "women do not have souls." (Smith & Haddad 2001: 39.) In that way, women became equated with animals, whose lives terminate forever after death. "The most basic relationship in Islamic society is not between man and woman, but between man and God: it is definitely not between woman and God." (Ibid.) The teachings of Islam about jawari, houris, and marriage show us that polygamy is understood by Muslim men as a means to satisfy man's craving for sensual pleasure. Woman, who is seen as inferior to the huri in everything, is considered an object of temporary entertainment and pleasure for man in this fleeting earthly life. The seventy-two virgins in Paradise are the eternal companions of man in the heavenly abode.

"You will never be able to be fair and just between women if it is your ardent desire." (Qur'an al-Nisa IV: 129). This verse very clearly stated that dealing justly between women in polygamy is not possible even if the husband strives diligently to do so. Modern scholars use this verse to argue, "that impartial treatment is not possible." (Yamani 1981 99.) In countries like Tunisia and Turkey, polygamy is illegal and most probably, legislators used verse like this to abolish the practice. Besides the subjective element, modernists use many factors to show that polygamy should not be practiced today. The most important factor is the problem of financing more than one household. As a condition, the Qur'an requires every husband to deal justly between his wives. For that reason, every wife would require her own house, property, and meeting other needs such as educating her children and providing for their better living. In our modern day, to do this is almost beyond a single man's means. Accordingly, in most of the Muslim societies today, polygamy is not a common practice.

Fatima Mernissi argued that although the Qur'an stated a condition for practicing polygamy, but the condition "is a subjective feeling, not easy to define legally." (Mernissi 1987: 47.) The Prophet Muhammad, himself admitted in a famous Hadith, known as "The Heart Inclination" that he was not able to deal justly between his wives. According to the Hadith, the Prophet loved his wife 'A'isha more than he loved his other wives. Scholars try to say that the Hadith speaks about love and not justice.

Factors that Encourage Polygamy in Muslim Societies: Besides the legal authorization of the practice by the Shari'a Law, there are other social factors encourage the practice in the Muslim societies. The most important of these factors are honor, barrenness, and circumcision of Muslim girls. Mernissi argued, "the concepts of honor and virginity locate the prestige of a man between the legs of a woman." (Mernissi 1988: 34.) When a woman fails to bleed because of penetration to break her hymen, is considered as a failure of social test, "she is taken back by the groom and his family to her own family." (Yamani 1981: 149.) In some cases, the husband might keep his wife, but marry another one to meet the virginity test. However, the first woman would be treated inferior to the second wife.

Circumcision of Girls in Islam: Circumcision of girls or Female Genital **Mutilation** is practiced in most Arab countries and more in countries like Sudan, Egypt, Eritrea, and Somalia. The practice is recommended by the Prophet and hence considered a Sunna. The main reason for the circumcision of girls, according to the jurists, is to restrain lust or the sex drive. For the girl nowadays is exposed to all kinds of temptations, they argue, which lead to depravity and corruption in society. According to the Prophet's statement, "Circumcision is a law for men and a preservation of honor for women." It is also believed by Muhammad that circumcision makes a woman more enjoyable, provided that it is practiced moderately. Umm 'Atiyya al-Ansarite narrated that a woman used to circumcise in Medina, and the Prophet said to her, "Do not overdo it, because this makes woman more favorable and it is more agreeable for the husband" (al-Bukhari, *Libas* 63, 64, *Isti'dsan* 51; Muslim, *Tahara* 49, Shaltut, *Khitan al-untha*, in

Liwa' al-Islam, 1951: 55).

Pharaonic or Sudanese circumcision "involves the removal or the sealing of the labia majora and the labia minora together after the entire clitoris has been removed." (Lois, 1985: 115.) Problem that result from female circumcision is that, "the woman no more capable of normal sexual intercourse and childbearing. And no longer able to gratify her spouse's appetite, she is cast out for younger and healthier wife." (Ibid: 117.) Again, in some cases, the husband might want to keep his wife for fear of her family or his reputation in the society, and marry another woman.

Chapter 10 Endnotes

[43] Muta'a means enjoyment. It is also a type of polygamous marriage.

[44] Ignorance. The period before Islam.

[45] Sexual intercourse.

[46] Swelling and firm, not sagging. (Haqq & Newton 1996: 16.)

[47] Ibn-Kathir, vol. 8, page 11, commentary on Q. 56:35-37, published by Dar Ash-sha'b, editorial footnote by the publisher explaining the meaning of 'dahman'.

Chapter Eleven

MUHAMMAD THE POLYGAMIST

The married life of the Prophet Muhammad puzzled many Muslims and Muslim scholars in our modern day. One of the main obligations of each Muslim writer is to justify the polygamous marriages of the Prophet. It is one of the main duties of every Muslim to imitate the example of the Prophet in every area of his life. For that reason, modern Muslim writers try always to find reasons to justify the marriages of the Prophet. The most commonly accepted reasons are summarized by the Egyptian writer Al-Sabooni under four topics. (Daagir 2002: 23)

1- <u>Educational reason</u>: The main reason for the Prophet having many wives was to produce female teachers to educate Muslim women in legal, social, and spiritual matters. Women found it difficult to consult the Prophet about personal problems such as menstruation, pregnancy, impurity, and marital issues.

2- <u>Legal reason</u>: To abolish some of al-Jahilia's customs such as the innovation of adoption. The Prophet married the wife of his adopted son to cancel this innovation.

3- <u>Social reason</u>: The Prophet married the daughters of his first and second caliphs, Abu Bakr and Omar, to unite socially the families of his close friends and successors.

4- <u>Political reason</u>: The Prophet married women from different tribes for tribal alliances.

Modern scholars like Muhammad Abdu and Rashid Rida accepted the four reasons of Al-Sabooni and added that, the only woman that the Prophet married for personal interests was his first wife Khadiga. Rida said that, "if the Prophet, peace and prayers be on him, wanted from women what kings and princes seek, pleasure and enjoyment, then he would not have married old widows and divorcees, but young and virgin women." (Ibid: 24.) According to Sabooni, the only virgin woman that Muhammad had married was the daughter of his best companion and successor, Abu Bakr, and that he did with the intention to reward his friend for his good deeds and appoint him as his first caliph. (Ibid.)

Mernissi rejected the assumption that most of the Prophet's marriages were done for the purpose of tribal alliances. (Mernissi 1987: 54). She argued that most of the Prophet's marriages were motivated by female's attraction and beauty. Examples of his marriages with Safiya Bint Huyay (a Jewish woman, whose tribe has been raided and defeated by Muhammad), Rayhana Bint Zayd (another Jewish woman), Maria the Coptic (a Christian girl, given as gift from Egypt to the Prophet),

Juwaryia Bint Al-Harith (she was so beautiful that whoever saw her fell in love with her), Zainab Bint Jahash (scandalous marriage, because she was the wife of his adopted son Zayd), and 'A'isha the daughter of his friend Abu Bakr (another problematic marriage because he married her when she was six years old and slept with her when she was nine)[48].

> *"The Prophet wrote the (marriage contract) with 'A'isha while she was six years old and consummated his marriage with her while she was nine years old and she remained with him for nine years (i.e. till his death)."* (Bukhari book 7, book 62, hadith No. 89.)

Rida admitted that he did not find any reason or wisdom behind the marriage of the Prophet to Mimona Bint Al-Harith (his last wife.) (Daagir 2002: 2). If we include Khadiga to the above list, we find that out of his sixteen wives, eight of them were married for reasons other than what the scholars believed. There is no verse in the Qur'an or Hadith, which says that the Prophet married his wives with the purpose of uniting the tribes together. On the contrary, there are many Hadiths in which the Prophet said, he loves women and perfume. (Ibid: 44.) The Prophet favored perfume because he believed that it increases sexual desire. For that reason, Muslim women were discouraged from wearing perfumes when they go out of their houses.

The Prophet praised his nephew, Hasan Ibn Ali, because Hasan was marriage addict. He married 200 wives (Mernissi 1987: 50). He used to divorce four wives at a time and marry another four. The Prophet said to him, "you resemble me physically and morally" (Ibid).

The Prophet himself failed to meet the condition of dealing justly between the women. The case of Maria the Coptic is a good example to show that the condition is an ideal and no man can fulfill it. The Prophet was caught by his wife Hafsa, having sexual intercourse with Maria in Safyia's house. When Hafsa informed Safyia, the later shouted angrily, "O Prophet of God, in my room, on my bed, and on my day? (Ibid: 55.)

'A'isha, the beloved wife of the Prophet, confessed that she hated the other wives of Muhammad and in some cases quarreled with them verbally and physically. One day she approached the Prophet with food in her hand. She found his wife, Sawadah Bint Zama'ah with him. She said to her, "eat before I cover your face with the food." When Sawadah did not respond, 'A'isha threw the food on her face. The Prophet laughed and told Sawadah to do the same thing to 'A'isha (al-Sabag 1981: 117).

Mernissi quoted two sayings of 'A'isha in which she admitted that polygamy brings hatred and jealousy between the wives. (Mernissi 1987: 55.)

"I never was as jealousy as I was of Maria. That is because she was a very beautiful, curly-haired woman. The Prophet was very attracted to her. In the beginning she was living near us and the Prophet spent entire days and nights with her until we protested and she became frightened."

"The Prophet was in my room when Juwariya came to ask him about a contract. By God, I hated her when I saw her coming towards him. I knew that he was going to see what I saw [her beauty]."

The Prophet admitted that polygamy harms the wife. When he came to know that his son-in-law, Ali Ibn Abi Talib was intended to marry another woman, he stood in the mosque at the Friday public prayer and said, *"I will not allow Ali Ibn Abi Talib and I repeat, I will not allow Ali to marry another woman except if he divorce my daughter. She is a part of me, and what harms her, harms me."* (Ibid: 70).

Polygamy is discouraged by some Modern Writers: Some modern Muslim writers like Dr. Nawal Al-Sa'dawi, Fatima Mernissi, and Gasm Amin discourage the practice of polygamy. As understood by Fatima Mernissi, "polygamy is a way for a man to humiliate the woman as a sexual being." (Ibid: 48.) It is commonly believed in Morocco, that the wife could be humiliated by marrying another woman beside her. The Sudanese people share the same opinion for they believed that, the best way to chastise the woman is to marry another woman with her. In Sudan and Egypt, the second wife is called Aldara, which means "Evildoer." Dr. Nawal Al-Sa'dawi saw that the oppression of Muslim women could be attributed to the patriarchal class system, which gives the Muslim man the right to enslave, oppress, and use the women for his own interests. (Yamani 1985: 83.) Gasm Amin argued that the verse of the Qur'an (al-Nisa 4:3) in fact discourages polygamy because the condition of dealing justly with the women cannot be fulfilled.

(Daagir 2002: 25.)

The married life of the Prophet Muhammad shows us that polygamy brings hatred, jealousy, quarrel, and family disorder. Moreover, the Prophet himself discouraged the practice when he forbade his son-in-law to marry another woman beside his daughter Fatima. If the Prophet is an ideal for every Muslim to imitate, then why not follow his example by discouraging the practice. Even the verse in the Qur'an cannot be taken as a license for practicing polygamy. It puts a condition, which the Prophet himself could not meet. Muslim countries like Tunisia and Turkey made the practice of polygamy punishable by the law. What the fundamentalists, in Egypt, called the Law of Jihan Al-Sada'at authorizes the wife to demand divorce, and keep the house, if her husband marries another woman when she is pregnant (Ibid). .

However, Muslim societies are not likely to give up those misogynistic traditions, which are full of hadiths that degraded women and considered them lower than animals. Besides that, the institution of marriage in Islam is nothing less than slavery system. Outstanding and distinguished scholars such as Saadawi and Ghazali admitted that marriage in Islam is a form of slavery. In her book, the Hidden Face of Eve, Sadaawi states: "The institution of marriage remained very different for men to what it was for women, and the rights accorded to husbands were distinct from those accorded to wives. In fact, it is probably not accurate to use the term 'rights of the woman' since a woman under the Islamic system of marriage has no human rights unless we consider that a slave has rights under a slave system. Marriage, in so far as women are concerned, is just like slavery to the slave, or the chains of serfdom to the serf." (Haqq & Newton 1996: 22.) Al-Imam al-Ghazali, who is considered the greatest Muslim ever lived after the Prophet, has summed his discussion about marriage in Islam in the following words: "The most satisfying and final word on the matter is that marriage is a form of slavery (riq). The woman is man's slave and her duty therefore is absolute obedience to the husband in all that he asks of her person. As Mohammad himself said: 'A woman, who at the moment of death enjoys the full approval of her husband, will find her place in Paradise'." (Ibid: 22.)

In conclusion, I would like to mention that the problem of Muslim women couldn't be solved through reformation or casting doubts on the traditions. Both efforts would not bring immediate solution to the problem of women. The majority of women are not likely to leave their religion or agree that some of their traditions are not authentic. They believe that the Qur'an and Hadith are divinely revealed and their teachings are divinely preserved. Nevertheless, they want to see that they are freed from the heavy weight of the Shari'a. In countries like Tunisia and Turkey, women achieved freedom and enjoy equality with men because the governments of those countries are not religiously based but secularly constituted. Religion in these countries became a private matter. The separation of religion from the state is the best solution for women in Muslim world. Laws in the form of Shari'a have given men the right to divorce their wives at will, beat their rebellious women, marry any number of women as they wish, deprive women from their rights to be educated or share in ruling the countries, and kill them for fear of loosing their honor. The founders of the Shari'a schools did not invent these laws. As we have seen that these laws are there in the religious texts (Qur'an and Hadith). No matter how we interpret them, they will still be used to justify those inhuman behaviors toward women. I don't believe a day will come when Muslim world will get rid of those misogynistic verses and hadiths. It is not likely to happen in a Muslim society where it is governed by the Shari'a laws that a man who marries more than one woman, beats his rebellious wife, or divorce his spouse at will that the law will prevent or punish him. Only under a secular Muslim government that women will be protected from such evil teachings.

Chapter 11 Endnotes

[48] Muhammad was 52 and 'A'isha was 9 when they married and sexually consummated their marriage.

Chapter Twelve

MUHAMMAD'S SCANDALOUS MARRIAGES

Under this heading I will discuss Muhammad's problematic relations with some of his women - his marriages to **'A'isha**, the daughter of his friend and first caliph, Abu Bakr, **Zainab Bint Jahash**, his cousin and the wife of his adopted son, Sayd, **Safiya Bint Huaya**, a Jewish-captive girl, and **Maria the Coptic**, a Christian female slave, given to him as a gift by the Maquoqis the king of Egypt.

Maria the Coptic was not counted by Muslim scholars as one of the wives of the Prophet or "Mothers of the faithful" because she remained a Christian and slave. She bore him a son, Ibrahim, who died in infancy. The Prophet's desire for Maria was described in a dramatic way by the books of the Sira.

Hafsa, one of the Prophet's wives, caught him having sexual intercourse with Maria in her room. "O Prophet of God, in my room and in my day!' shouted Hafsa angrily. Afraid of the anger of his other wives, and especially of his most beloved 'A'isha, he promised Hafsa never to touch Maria again if she would keep the matter secret. But she spoke out, and the matter reached the ears of 'A'isha. When his beloved 'A'isha confronted him he received a revelation from heaven which justified and legalized his action with Maria (Sura 66:3).

Muhammad's strong desire for Maria the Coptic is best described in 'A'isha's words: "I never was as jealous as I was of Maria. That is because she was a very beautiful, curly haired woman. The Prophet was very attracted to her. In the beginning, she was living near us and the Prophet spent entire days and nights with her until we protested and she became frightened." (Ibn Sa'ad, al-Tabaqat: 212).

The Prophet then decided to transfer Maria to a more secure dwelling far from his legitimate wives and continued his sexual relation with her in spite of their protest. .

Maria became pregnant and delivered a baby-boy whom the Prophet named Ibrahim "or Abraham." When Aisha saw the baby she told the Prophet that the child did not resemble him. Then a rumor reached the Prophet's ears that Maria was in fact impregnated by the man who brought her from Egypt and that Ibrahim was not his own son. Muhammad outraged and sent Ali to strike off the neck of the man. However, the man was escaped the death penalty when it appeared that he was not capable of having sexual intercourse "or eunuch and his penis was cut off" (Sahih Muslim, hadith no. 4975). Muhammad did not follow the same principle when his beloved 'A'isha was accused of having sex with Safwan Ibn al-Mu'atal.

Safiya Bint Huaya was the daughter of Huaya, one of the Jewish leaders. When Muhammad invaded Khibar, the Jewish city, he killed Safiya's husband, father, and uncle. Her husband was Canana Bin al-Rabi'a, whom the Prophet tortured to death and extracted from him the hiding place of his treasure. In the beginning Safiya was taken as slave-captive by Dhaia al-Kaleb. When the news reached the Prophet's ears that Safiya was extremely beautiful and the daughter of a Jewish leader, he took her from Dhaia. Safiya reported to have said, "I have never hated any man more than the Prophet, because he killed my husband, father, and all my people." The Prophet gave Safiya three days to mourn her people before he slept with her. On the third night she begged him to give her more time to morn her relatives. However, the Prophet said, he would not wait any longer. Therefore, he stopped his camel and ordered his men to erect for him a tent to sleep with Safiya. Abu Huraira narrated: "While the Messenger of God was consummating the marriage with Safiyya, Abu Ayyub spent the night at the door of the Prophet. When the Messenger of God woke up and he said, "Allahu akbar," there was a sword with Abu Ayyub. Abu Ayyub said, "O Messenger of God, she was a newly married woman, and you killed her father, brother, and husband, so I did not feel secure about you with her." The Messenger of God laughed and said, "It all went well." (The story of Safiya was mentioned in details in al-Sira al-Halabia, Ibn Hisham, and Tabaqat Ibin Sa'ad). The Islamic sources stated that Safiya became a Muslim later on and the Prophet married her. For that reason she is included among the Mothers of the Faithful.

Zainab Bint Jahash: The marriage of Zainab was described by Fatima Mernessi as scandalous marriage because Zainab was the wife of the Prophet's adopted son, Zayd. She was the wife of Muhammad's adopted son, Zayd, and therefore, in the eyes of the Arabs, as good as his own daughter-in-law. Muhammad went to her house when her husband was away, saw her in a state of seminudeness, and was aroused. According to the Sira, God sent a wind, which lifted up the curtain of the tent and Muhammad saw Zainab lying on her bed half-naked. Zainab is described by the Sira as fair, beautiful, and has lovely body.

When Zayd heard about it, he offered to divorce her, but Muhammad, fearing a public scandal, told him to keep his wife for himself. At this point Allah spoke and decided the matter (Qur'an 33:36-40). He blamed Muhammad for telling Zayd, "Retain thou in wedlock thy wife," and for hiding in his heart "that which God was about to make manifest." Allah told Muhammad: "Thou feared the people, but it is more fitting that thou should fear God," and He revealed His plan, present and future, to Muhammad thus: "We joined her in marriage to thee, in order that in future there may be no difficulty to the believers in the matter of marriage with the wives of their adopted sons." He now also addressed Himself to the Muslims of all generations: "It is not fitting for a believer, man or woman, when a matter has been decided by God and His Apostle to have any option about their decision. If anyone disobeys God and His Apostle, he is indeed clearly on a wrong path." Based on this marriage it became a law that if Muhammad sees any woman and desires her it becomes compulsory for her husband to divorce her at once and she becomes the wife of the Prophet! Moreover, the Qur'an mentioned that if any woman wants to offer herself to the Prophet and Muhammad wants to have Nikah with her he alone among the believers is allowed to do so. Muhammad also is exempted from the restriction of the Qur'an that a man should marry only four women at a time. In other words, the Prophet alone is allowed to have any number of wives and that is why he married sixteen women and two concubines (Maria and Rayhana)..

Muhammad made Zayd himself go to his wife with his marriage proposal. "Allah's Messenger said to Zayd to make a mention to her about him." The marriage ordered from above was celebrated with unusual festivity. "Allah's Messenger gave no better wedding feast than the one he did on the occasion of his marriage with Zainab."

The Hadiths and the Commentators: Muhammad Ibn Yahya Ibn Hayyan narrated, "The Messenger of God came to Zayd's house seeking him. [Zayd was then called Zayd Ibn Muhammad]. Perhaps the Messenger of God missed him at that time that is why he said, 'Where is Zayd?' He went to his house seeking him and, when he did not find him, Zainab Bint Jahsh stood up to [meet] him in a lighthouse dress, but the Messenger of God turned away from her. She said, 'He is not here, Messenger of God, so please come in; my father and mother are your ransom.' The Messenger of God refused to come in. Zainab had hurried to dress herself when she heard that the Messenger of God was at her door, so she leapt in a hurry, and the Messenger of God was deeply moved by her when she did that. He went away muttering something that was hardly understandable but for this sentence: 'Praise be to God who disposes the hearts.' When Zayd came back home, she told him that the Messenger of God came. Zayd asked, 'You asked him to come in, didn't you?' She replied, 'I bade him to, but he refused.' He said, 'Have you heard [him say] anything?' She answered, 'When he had turned away, I heard him say something that I could hardly understand. I heard him say, "Praise be to God who directs the hearts." 'Zayd went out to the Messenger of God and said, 'O Messenger of God, I learned that you came to my house. Did you come in? O Messenger of God, my father and mother are your ransom. Perhaps you liked Zainab. I can leave her.' The Messenger of God said, 'Hold on to your wife.' Zayd said, 'O Messenger of God, I will leave her.' The Messenger of God said, 'Keep your wife.' So when Zayd left her, she isolated herself and finished her legal period. While the Messenger of God was sitting talking with 'A'isha, he was taken in a trance, and when it was lifted, he smiled and said, 'Who will go to Zainab to tell her the good news that God wedded her to me from heaven?' The Messenger of God recited, 'Thus you told someone whom God had favoured and whom you yourself have favoured: "Hold on to your wife?" ' 'A'isha said, "I heard a great deal about her beauty and, moreover, about how God wedded her from heaven, and I said, 'For sure she will boast over this with us.' Salama, the slave of the Messenger of God, came out running and I told her about that. She gave me some silver jewellery for her." Zainab Bint Umm Salama narrated, "I heard my mother, Umm Salama, say, 'I once mentioned Zainab Bint Jahsh and asked for God's mercy upon her soul, and narrated some of the things that happened between her and 'A'isha. Zainab said, "By God, I am unlike any of the wives of the Messenger of God; he was given them in marriage by dowries and needed guardians to wed them. As for me, it was God who wedded me to the Messenger of God and revealed the scripture on my account; Muslims will continue to read with no change or alteration- 'Thus you told someone whom God had favoured.' Umm Salama said, "The Messenger of God found her desirable and used to visit her frequently. She was a good woman and used to fast regularly, did good and gave her money away to the needy".

The books of the Prophet's Sira narrate that Muhammad sent Zayd to propose to her. Anas narrated: "When the legal period of Zainab Bint Jahsh was finished, the Messenger of God said to Zayd Ibn Haritha, 'I have none that I can trust, other than myself, but you. Go to Zainab and propose to her for me.' So Zayd went off and came to her while she was leavening dough. Zayd said, 'When I saw her, she became greater in heart, and I could not look at her since I knew that the Messenger of God mentioned her. So I turned my back on her and said, "O Zainab, rejoice; the Messenger of God has mentioned you." She said, 'I shall do nothing until I ask the advice of my Lord.' She rose up and went to pray [or to her mosque]. Then the verse was revealed: 'Once Zayd has accomplished his purpose with her, We married her off to you.' Then the Messenger of God came and entered without permission."

'A'isha Bint Abu Bakr: She was Muhammad's third wife. 'A'isha herself narrated, "The Messenger of God married me in Shawwal in the tenth year after of his prophet-hood, three years before the Migration as I was six years old. I was nine years old when he consummated the marriage with me. Ibn Hisham holds that "Muhammad married her when she was seven years old and consummated the marriage with her when they were in Medina when she was nine years old. The Messenger of God did not marry any other virgin but her. 'A'isha narrated, "The Messenger of God married me when I was still playing with the girls. I did not know that the Messenger of God married me until my mother took me and locked me up in the house. Then I realised that I was married." There is another tradition by 'Atiyya: "The Messenger of God proposed to 'A'isha Bint Abi Bakr while she was a little girl. Abu Bakr said, 'O Messenger of God, can a man marry his brother's daughter?' Muhammad replied, 'You are my brother in my religion.' So he [Abu Bakr] married her off for the chattel of a house, fifty [dirhams] worth, or so." "I was playing with the girls during the lifetime of the Messenger of God. The Messenger of God came to me when I was playing with the girls, and asked me, 'What is this, 'A'isha?' I said, 'The horses of Solomon.' He laughed."

'A'isha said, "I am held superior to the wives of the Prophet for ten things." She was asked, "What are they, mother of believers?" She replied, "He did not marry any virgin but me, he did not marry someone whose parents were migrants [that is from Makka to Medina] but me. God revealed my innocence [of adultery] from heaven, and

Gabriel brought him my image in a piece of silk and said, 'Marry her; she is your wife.' So I used to bathe with him from the same receptacle. He never did that with anyone else but me. He used to pray while I was lying between his hands, which is something that he never let any of his other wives do. The inspiration used to come down upon him while he was with me. He passed away when he was in my bosom during the night when he was supposed to have intercourse with me, and he was buried in my home."

Once `A'isha asked the Prophet, "Who will be your wives in paradise?" He answered, "You will be one of them." We learn from the stories that `A'isha was Muhammad's favourite wife. `Amr Ibn al-`As asked him, "O Messenger of God, who is your favourite among people?" He replied, "`A'isha." `Amr said, "I meant male ones." He answered, "Her father." And lastly, we mention the following, "The superiority of `A'isha to other women is like the superiority of tarid [a meal of bread and meat] to other kinds of food." Another tradition says that he died before he had enough of tarid `A'isha was eighteen years old when the Prophet died. She remained a widow until the age of sixty-two. Based on a verse in the Qur'an Muhammad's wives are not allowed to be married to any man after his death.

"I would be playing with my dolls," narrated `A' isha, "with the girls who were my friends, and the Prophet would come in and they would slip out of the house and he would go out after them and bring them back, for he was pleased for my sake to have them there." Sometimes he would say "Stay where you are" before they had time to leave, and would also join in their games. 'A'isha said: "One day, the Prophet came in when I was playing with the dolls and he said: 'O 'A'isha, whatever game is this?' 'It is Solomon's horses,' I said and he laughed." Sometimes as he came in he would screen himself with his cloak so as not to disturb 'A'isha and her friends.

The Prophet married Malika Bint Ka'b who was known for her resplendent, magnificent beauty. 'A'isha entered to her and said, "Are you not ashamed of marrying the killer of your father?" So Malika took refuge with God from the Prophet, and he divorced her" (Tabaqat Ibn Sa'ad, 8:141; Usd al-ghaba, 5:525).

Aisha accused the Prophet that whenever he wants to sleep with a woman he brings a verse and claims that God revealed it to him. In that regard Aisha remarked, "It seems to me that your Lord hastens to satisfy your desire." (Sahih Muslim vol.2:3453-3454 p.748-749). It is not clear on what occasion Aisha made such a doubting remark. Some source referred it to the incident when the Prophet was caught by his wife Hafsa in the very act of having sex with his slave girl Maria the Coptic, other source related it to his scandalous marriage with his daughter-in-law, Zainab bint Jahsh, and yet other source to the women who offered themselves to the Prophet.

Aisha accused of adultery:

Narrated Ibn Aun: *I wrote a letter to Nafi and Nafi wrote in reply to my letter that the Prophet had suddenly attacked Bani Mustaliq without warning while they were heedless and their cattle were being watered at the places of water. Their fighting men were killed and their women and children were taken as captives; the Prophet got Juwairiya on that day. Nafi said that Ibn 'Umar had told him the above narration and that Ibn 'Umar was in that army.*

In this Ghazwat "or invasion" Aisha was with Mohammad and she was not happy about the fact that Mohammad in a short period has had married himself two new women, one Zainab (former wife of Zayd) and now Juwairiya. According to Aisha, on the way back to Medina in one of the stops, she goes out to answer the call of nature but she does not return to her howdah[49] in time so she remains behind all alone in the desert. Which means her slaves would have mounted the howdah on the camel without looking inside or feeling the weight difference without Aisha being in it. At that time Aisha was only 15 years old.

Aisha waits there until Safwan bin Al-Muattal As-Sulami, a handsome young man and the rear-guard of Mohammad's army arrives and finds her sleeping all-alone in the desert. There is a detailed description of his actions: he recites a Qur'anic verse to express his surprise then he makes his camel kneel and puts his legs over the front legs of the camel to hold it down for 'Aisha to mount it. 'Aisha does not mention any conversation between them, as if she did not explain to him what had happened. But in other hadiths (e.g. in hadith no. 188 in Bukhari) there is plenty of evidence of lively conversations they normally had from behind the veil, and even though the situation of being alone with this man in the desert called for extra-reserved manners, it is more likely that in the light of later accusations 'Aisha would not mention any action which could inspire even a spark of suspicion.

'Aisha and Safwan arrived the next morning to Medina. Due to the strong rivalry between Zainab and Aisha, Zainab accuses Aisha of infidelity with Safwan. At the same time Abdullah bin Ubai and Hamna bint Jahsh (Zainab's sister) spread the rumor all over the Medina that 'Aisha committed adultery with Safwan.

Aisha says: "I became ill for a month. The people were propagating the forged statements of the slanderers while I was unaware of anything of all that, but I felt that in my present ailment, I was not receiving the same kindness from Allah's Apostle as I used to receive when I got sick. (But now) Allah's Apostle would only come, greet me and say,' How is that (lady)?' and leave. That roused my doubts."

According to Aisha, she was ill and was staying with her parents during that time and had no idea about the rumors. She first found out about it after a month. It seems that Mohammad wasn't happy with her at that time so that's why she was staying with her parents. In the meantime Mohammad was trying to find out the truth about this rumour. He ordered Ali to interrogate Barira (Aisha's female-slave) to find out more about whereabouts of Aisha on that night. According to Tabari, Ali even beat Barira up in front of Mohammad but with no result.

The questions that come to mind are: Didn't Aisha's slaves realize that the howdah was empty? Couldn't Safwan ride faster to get Aisha to the army? Isn't the duty of the rear-guard to get to the army in time and warn them of an attack?

Feeling suspicious Mohammad went to Abu Bakr house to speak to Aisha. Aisha assured him of her innocent and on the spot Mohammad went into trance. He got up and explained that Allah has spoken to him and has revealed the surah an-Nur, which contains the laws and punishments for adultery.

At the end three people received punishment for spreading the rumor, Hassan bin Thabit, Mistah bin Uthatha and Hamna bint Jahsh, 80 stripes each. (Qur'an: an-Nur 24: 4). *"And those who accuse honourable women but bring not four witnesses, scourge them (with) eighty stripes and never (afterward) accept their testimony - They indeed are evil-doers"* (Qur'an an-Nur 24: 4).

Surprisingly Muhammad waited so long until he received a revelation from heaven justifying 'Aisha. In case of Maria the Coptic, he believed at once the rumor of her affair with the other slave-man and sent 'Ali to kill him The Qur'an requires the witness of two men in every accusation except adultery. Since the accusation of Aisha it became almost impossible to prove adultery in Islam. Besides four witnesses, the Shari'a requires that the witnesses should bring a thread and pass it between the adulterer and the adulteress. If the thread could not pass between them then that proves the man's penis is inside the woman's vagina.

Wives and Concubines of Muhammad:[50]

1. Khadija bint Khuwailid - died first
2. Sawda bint Zam'a
3. Aisha bint Abu Bakr
4. Umm Salama
5. Hafsa bint Umar.
6. Zainab bint Jahsh
7. Juwairiyya bint al-Harith
8. Omm Habiba
9. Safiya bint Huaya
10. Maimuna bint al-Harith
11. Fatima (briefly)
12. Ramlah the daughter of Abu Sufyan[51]
13. Asma of Saba
14. Zainab al-Khozayma
15. Habla
16. Asma bint al-Nu'man

Slaves / Concubines

17. Maria the Coptic
18. Rayhana bint Zayd

Chapter 12 Endnotes

[49] A small tent-like that Muslim women sit inside while they are traveling on a camel's back.

[50] Muhammad and his wives. Persian Journal, September 7, 2005.

D:\Documents and Settings\occ\Desktop\Muhammad & His Wives, So Many of Them - Persian Journal Latest Iran news & Iranian Newspaper.htm

[51] Ramlah bint Abu Sufyan, the daughter of Abu Sufyan. She was married to prophet Muhammad one year after the Hijra. Her first husband, Ubayd-Allah ibn Jahsh, the brother of Zaynab bint Jahsh, were among the first people to accept Islam. Both emigrated to Abyssinia (Ethiopia) in order to be safe.

There she gave birth to her daughter, Habibah bint Ubayd-Allah.

There her husband converted back to his previous religion, Christianity, the religion of the Abyssinians.

Chapter Thirteen

MUHAMMAD THE RAIDER

In his book, *Shukran…Bin Laden (Thanks…Bin Laden),* al-Qimni explains in more detail the philosophy of the Islamic Jihad. According to him, Islam "divides the world into two parts: (Dar al-Islam)[52] which are the lands of peace and security that include the Muslim countries, and (Dar al-Hareb)[53] which include all the countries of the world that Muslim army can attack any time whenever there is good chance to do so" (al-Qimni 2004: 190). The obligation of Jihad began after Muhammad and his followers fled from Makka to Medina.

Our history says to us, after the immigration of Muslims from Makka to Yathrib/Medina, where the alliances of the Prophet and Banu Hashim from the most able warriors of the tribes of Awas and Khazirq, where the Jewish factories of weapons, and where the good geographic location. The

Muslims started attacking the Makkans and the rest of the Arabs. This happened in the form of organized and continuous invasions and attacks… The first attacking group was led by Abd Allah ibn Jahsh[54] in which he violated the conditions of the holy months. The group killed, robbed, and took captives from that Makkan caravan. Those attacks and robberies continued in the Arabian Peninsula until turned to Islamic invasions to other countries of the world. In all their battles the Muslims were always the attackers except in two battles: the Battle of Uhud and the Battle of the Ditch[55] (Ibid: 190-191).

Osama bin Zayd led another campaign in order to terrorize the Romans **"for terrorism was one of the important pillars of Islam and its means to victory"** (Ibid: 192, emphasis is mine). While Osama bin Zayd preparing his troops to invade the Roman lands, the Prophet commanded him "to attack them in the darkness of the dawn and fall on them killing and burn them with fire and invade them and return with the booties" (al-Qimni 2004: 191-192, see Ibn Habib in al-Mahabir p 117, Ibn Kathir in al-Bedaiah wa al-Nihaiah p 139, 143, Ibn Said al-Nas in 'Auion al-Atharig p 145, al-Suhili in Rawd Alanif p 24, Ibn Hisham p 245, and al-Tabari in Tarikh al-Rusul wa al-Milook p 156). In order to support his point, al-Qimni quoted the Prophet's hadiths in which he said," I have granted victory through terrorism… I have been sent with the Sword between my hands so that no one should be worshipped except Allah…My living is under the tip of my Spear… I have commanded to fight people until they bear witness that there is no God but Allah and Muhammad is the Messenger of Allah" (Ibid). The Qur'an also supported the sayings of the Prophet in the following verses:

> *And those of the People of the Book who aided them - Allah did take them down from their strongholds and* **cast terror into their hearts***. (So that) some ye slew, and some ye made prisoners* (Qur'an al-Ahzab 33: 26, emphasis is mine).

> *Soon shall* **We cast terror into the hearts of the Unbelievers,** *for that they joined companions with Allah, for which He had sent no authority: their abode will be the Fire: And evil is the home of the wrongdoers!* (Qur'an Ali-Umran 3: 151, emphasis is mine).

> *The punishment of those who wage war against Allah and His Messenger, and strive with might and main for mischief through the land is:* **execution, or crucifixion, or the cutting off of hands and feet from opposite sides, or exile from the land***: that is their disgrace in this world, and a heavy punishment is theirs in the Hereafter;* (Qur'an al-Maidah 5: 34, emphasis is mine).

According to Sayyid al-Qimni "The Islamic army attacked the tribes in the Arabian Peninsula and subjected them by force to its new State, after terrorizing them so that they have to join the Medinian alliance" (al-Qimni 1996: 235). Al-Qimni gave many examples to show how Muhammad terrorized the Arabs and the Jewish tribes and subjected them by the sword to his new State. "The Arabs of Bani

Salim that great tribe fled from their dwelling places as soon as they heard about the approaching Islamic troops. They left behind their houses and cattle. The Muslims stayed three days in their houses and returned to Yathrib with great booty" (Ibid).

The Prophet Muhammad always gets the 1/5 of the booty (Qur'an al-Anfaal 41). The share of the Prophet was decided for the first time by his uncle "Abd Allah ibn Jahsh[56] in his attack on the Battle of al-Nakhala. That battle in, which he violated the forbidden months and captured the booty of the caravan. It was the first plunder for the Muslims. Abd Allah said, 'the 1/5 in everything we loot is for the Messenger of Allah and the rest should be divided between us.' A qur'anic revelation came after that confirming what the uncle of the Prophet has decided" (Ibid: 236, Qur'an al-Anfaal 41).

After the Battle of Badr, "It became clear to the Arabs that the attitudes of the Muslims have changed. The Muslims began to go out in ceaseless military campaigns to cut the alliances to Makka, and the inside trade roads, and attacking the tribes in their dwelling places to terrorize them so that they should cut their alliances with Makka, and subject them by force to the Islamic State" (Ibid: 238).

Commenting on some verses of the Qur'an (al-Baqarah 191, 193, al-Nisa 76, 89, 91, al-Touba 12, 14, 29, and al-Anfaal 39) Khalil Abdul-Karim states,

These verses carry serious orders of killing the tribes that refuse to believe in the faith that is preached by Muhammad… And from the other side there are hadiths issued by the

Prophet that confirm this meaning very clearly by which we mean killing any one refuses Islam 'I have been commanded to fight the people until they bear witness that there is no God except Allah and Muhammad is the Messenger of Allah, if they say it they uphold from me their wealth and bloods.' The meaning of noncompliance is that any one refuses to witness or utter the two Shihadah[57] there would be no protection for his wealth and blood ... Accordingly killing the one who refuses to utter the two Shihadah (indicating his acceptance to Islam) is an obligation to every Muslim without exception... The message of Muhammad to all the tribes is 'accept Islam and you will be safe'... Any tribe or an individual refuses this offer would expose themselves/himself to physical annihilation and theirs/his wealth, women, and slave-girls would be taken by the Muslims (Abdul-Karim 1999: 42-44).

After the victory of the Battle of Badr the new verses of the Qur'an began to abrogate the old verses of the Qur'an that gave freedom of faith to everyone. For thirteen years Muhammad preached his new religion in Makka and gained only seventy converts. During that period the Qur'an stated very clearly "there is no compulsion in religion." However, after the victory of Badr Muhammad turned one hundred and eighty degree and began to dictate new religion. The Qur'an forbade the freedom of faith and Islam became the only acceptable religion to God. Anyone refuses to accept Islam would be executed and his property, cattle, women, and children would be distributed among the Muslim troops. However, the Jews and the Christians (i.e. the People of the Book) somehow were exempted with some conditions.

For the Jews and Christians the Qur'an states: *"Fight those who believe neither in Allah nor the Last day, nor hold the forbidden which hath been forbidden by Allah and his messenger, nor acknowledge the Religion of Truth from among the People of the Book,*[58] *until they pay the Jiziyah with willing submission. And feel themselves subdued" (Qur'an: At-Touba 9:29).* Islam requires complete submission from the Jews and the Christians. At that time the Jews were seen as great threat to the new religion because "they have heavenly Book and religious constitution and this matter made them to be the living heavenly denial to the prophecy of the Arab Prophet who claims that his religion comes from the same sources as that of the Jewish. Therefore, the existence of the Jews in Arabia became permanent and real threat to the new State and its ideologies" (Ibid: 243). Accordingly it became necessary "to expel them from Yathrib and cut their roots. And this matter was carried out without delay and without compromise" (Ibid). Thus, followed the massacres and expulsion of the Jews from Medina. The same massacres would have been done to the Christians if they happened to be in Medina. For the Qur'an equates the Christians with the Jews because it sees them friends to each other and great threat to his claim to be Prophet.

*O you who believe! Take not the Jews and
the Christians for friends. They are friends one
to another. He among you who taketh them
for friends is one of them. Lo Allah guideth
not wrongdoing folk (Qur'an al-Ma'idah 5: 51).*

*The Jews call 'Uzayr-a son of God', and the Christians call 'Christ
the Son Of God'. That is a saying from their mouth; (In this) they but
intimate what the unbelievers of old used to say. Allah's curse be on
them: how they are deluded away from the Truth (Qur'an al-touba
9: 30).*

For the Arab tribes and later on the entire world the Qur'an states:
*"But when the forbidden months are past, then fight and slay the Pagans
wherever ye find them, and seize them, beleaguer them, and lie in wait
for them in every stratagem (of war); but if they repent, and establish
regular prayers and practise regular charity, then open the way for them:
for Allah is Oft-Forgiving, Most Merciful" (Qu'an: At-Touba 9: 5).* As
we mentioned earlier, this verse is known as "**THE VERSE OF THE
SWORD**" This single verse abrogated or cancelled **123 verses of the
Qur'an.** Any earlier verse that speaks about peace and freedom of
faith is nullified and became dead by this verse. Today many Muslims
claimed that Islam is a religion of Peace and in order to prove their
point they always quote those abrogated verses such as

"But there is no compulsion in religion" (Surah 2:256),

*"He who obeys the Messenger, obeys Allah: but if any turn away, we
have not sent thee to watch over their (evil deeds)" (Surah 4:80),*

"And dispute ye not with the People of the Book, except with means better (than mere disputation), unless it be with those of them who inflict wrong (and injury); but say, 'We believe in the revelation which has come down to us and in that which came down to you; our God and your God is One; and it is to Him we bow (in Islam)" *(Surah 29:46).*

"Fight in the cause of Allah those who fight you, but do not transgress limits; for Allah loveth not transgressors" (Surah 2:190)

"So if they dispute with thee, say: 'I have submitted my whole self to Allah and so have those who follow me,' And say to the People of the Book and so to those who are unlearned: 'do ye (also) submit yourself? If they do, they are in right guidance, but if they turn back, thy duty is to convey the Message" (Surah 3:20).

Below is a list of the Qur'anic Verses that have been abrogated (nullified) by **the Verse of the Sword:** -

Surah 5: 99
Surah 2:62
Surah 2:109
Surah 5:13
Surah 6:70
Surah 8:61
Surah 2:83
Surah 2:139
Surah 2:191
Surah 2:192
Surah 3:28
Surah 4:63
Surah 4:80
Surah 4:81
Surah 4:84
Surah 4:90
Surah 5:2
Surah 6: 66; 104; 106- 108; 112; 135; 158

Surah 7:183; 199
Surah 10: 41, 46, 99, 108, 109
Surah 11: 121
Surah 13: 40
Surah 15: 3, 85, 88, 94
Surah 16: 82, 125, 127
Surah 17: 54
Surah 19: 84
Surah 20: 130, 135
Surah 22: 68
Surah 23: 54, 96
Surah 24: 54
Surah 28: 55
Surah 30: 60
Surah 32: 30
Surah 33:48
Surah 34: 25
Surah 39: 15
Surah 41: 34
Surah 42: 6, 15, 48
Surah 43: 83, 89
Surah 44: 59
Surah 45: 14
Surah 46: 35
Surah 50: 39
Surah 52: 48
Surah 53: 29
Surah 58: 8-9, 11
Surah 73: 10
Surah 76: 8
Surah 86: 17
Surah 88: 22- 24
Surah 109: 6

Some Muslims and Muslim scholars today try to show that Islam is a religion of peace, love, patience, tolerance, and grant freedom of faith. In order to prove their point they quote the above verses of the Qur'an. However, all the above verses were written in Makka when Muhammad was weak and had less number of followers (seventy converts). Those verses are known as the Makkan verses because they are believed to be revealed to the Prophet in Makka. The verses that forbade freedom of faith and made Islam is the only acceptable religion to Allah are known as the Medinian verses. Following are samples of those Medinian verses that made Islam is the only acceptable religion to Allah:

If anyone desires a religion other than Islam (submission to Allah., never will it be accepted of him; and in the Hereafter He will be in the ranks of those who have lost (All spiritual good). (Ali-Umaran 3: 85).

Do they seek for other than the Religion of Allah.-while all creatures in the heavens and on earth have, willing or unwilling, bowed to His Will (Accepted Islam), and to Him shall they all be brought back (Ali-Umaran 3: 83).

The Religion before Allah is Islam (submission to His Will): (Ali-Umaran 3 19).

"And fight them until there is no more Fitnah (disbelief and polytheism, i.e. worshipping others besides Allah), and the religion (worship) will all be for Allaah Alone [in the whole of the world]" (al-Anfaal 8:39).

"Then when the Sacred Months (the 1st, 7th, 11th, and 12th months of the Islamic calendar) have passed, then kill the Mushrikoon (see V.2:105) wherever you find them, and

capture them and besiege them, and lie in wait for them in each and every ambush. But if they repent [by rejecting Shirk (polytheism) and accept Islamic Monotheism] and perform As-Salaah (Iqaamat-as-Salaah), and give Zakaah, then leave their way free. Verily, Allaah is Oft-Forgiving, Most Merciful" (at-Touba 9:5). **Ayat al-Sayf (the verse of the sword).**

The Battle of Badr: Muhammad and his followers fought many battles the most famous of them are the Battle of Badr and the Battle of Uhud. In Badr Muslims defeated the Makkans whereas in Uhud they received a crashing defeat. Muhammad and his followers failed to intersect the caravan of Abu Sufyan, the leader of the Makkans, while on his way to al-Sham or "Syria" (Ibid: 1996: 154, quoting al-Halabi, al-Sira, p. 374). Muslims wanted to attack the caravan of the Makkans and take the booty. By this time, Muhammad began raiding the Arab tribes and their caravans. However, Muslims discovered that their calculations were wrong when they reached the place where they expected to find the caravan (Ibid). Abu Sufyan was able to reach safely to al-Sham with his caravan.

Muhammad did not give up and wait for the return of Abu Sufyan with the caravan. When the Makkans knew that Muhammad and his men went out of Medina to attack the caravan, they came out with many fighters. Once again Abu Sufyan was able to deceive Muhammad and pass with the caravan without being attacked. When the Makkan fighters knew that Abu Sufyan was able to pass with his caravan without being attacked, they decided, "to celebrate the safety of their monies and spread their honour" (Ibid: 175). However, Muhammad being deceived twice by Abu Sufyan decided to attack the Makkan fighters. The Muslims were three hundred fighters while the Makkans were one thousand. There is no way for the Muslims to defeat the Makkans if they came face to face with them. For that reason they decided to give them a surprise attack. On the other camp, the Makkans did not expect the Muslims to attack them. Therefore, they began to celebrate by drinking and dancing. When the Muslims attacked them they were already very drunk and unarmed. According to alsirah al-halabia, "Qurash stood with great astonishment, after its celebration was turned from drums and singing and drinking wine to war and blood" (Ibid: 180, quoting al-Halabi, alsirah, p. 395).

Although, the reason for the defeat of the Makkans and the victory of the Muslims is obvious, the Muslim historians attributed the victory to some fighting angels "Abu Imamat said to his son, 'oh my son in the day of Badr, when one of us points his sword towards the unbeliever, his head falls off his body before the sword reach him" (Ibid: 208, quoting al-Tabari p. 453). Ibn Abass states,

> While a man from the Muslims was running after the heels of a man from the unbelievers, he heard a sound of a whip over his head and the voice of the knight saying: come forward oh Haizum (and Hizum is the horse of the angel Gabriel). When the unbeliever looked in front of him he fell flat on the ground. When we looked at him we saw his nose

was bleeding and his face was cut due to the strike of the whip. He turned into green colour. The ansari man came and informed the Messenger of Allah with all that. The Prophet said: 'you told the truth. That was the support from the third heaven (Ibid. quoting from al-Bihaqi pp. 51-52).

Ibn al-Rawandi asks "**where those angels in the day of Uhud** when the Prophet hid himself among the dead and no one supported him?" (Ibid: 211, quoting Ibrahim Biuomi in the Islamic Philosophy, p. 83, emphasis in the original).

The Battle of Uhud: The victory of Badr gave Muslims great confidence and led them to carry out many attacks on the other Arab and Jewish tribes. The Qur'an assures the Muslims that Allah is fighting with them and that by sending his angels to engage in combat with their enemies. There are many verses in the Qur'an to confirm that many angels joined the Muslims in the Battle of Badr and defeated the Makkans.

> *When thou didst say unto the believers: Is it not sufficient for you that your Lord should support you with three thousand angels sent down (to your help)? (Qur'an 3: 124).*
>
> *When ye sought help of your Lord and He answered you (saying): I will help you with a thousand of the angels, rank on rank (Qur'an 8: 9).*

However, in the Battle of Uhud the Muslims received a crashing defeat and Muhammad himself was beaten badly and seriously wounded. There was a promise in the Qur'an that Allah would support Muslim fighters with three or five thousands fighting-angels in the Battle of Uhud (Ali-Umaran 121, 125, 151). Unfortunately this promise was not fulfilled and Muslims were defeated. According to Ibn Kathir, al-Halabi, and al-Bihaqi the defeat of Uhud came as result of the Muslim fighters deserting their posts and running after the beautiful Makkan women. "I swear by Allah I saw the wealthy Makkan women running and climbing the mountain and their ornaments and legs appeared because **they had lifted up their clothes** to reveal their legs. The men with Abd Allah bin Zubiar, the fighters shouted to one another, let us go after **the booty**, and let us go after the Makkan women. Therefore, the fighters ran after the legs and the booty and deserted their defensive position" (Ibid: 259, quoting from Al-Halabi p. 502, Ibn Kathir p 23, and al-Bihaqi p 229, emphasis on the original). The retreat of the Makkan fighters and the women revealing their ornaments and beautiful legs was a trap for the Muslims (Ibid: 260). The Makkans understood the psychology of the Muslim fighters. Most of them joined Muhammad for the material gains such as wealth and women. Therefore, they tricked them that they were defeated and that they and their women were running away from the battlefield. When the Muslim fighters deserted their defensive position and ran after the women, the hidden Makkan troops that led by Khalid bin al-Walid who was still unbeliever, and Akramah bin Abu Jahal ambushed the Muslims "who were busy in robbery and stealing" (Ibid). The unexpected attack of the Makkans caused great confusion among the Muslims, which led them to strike one another unknowingly (Ibid, quoting al-Halabi p 205). Khalid's troops began to attack the Muslim fighters and kill some of them. When the fighting became tough the Muslim fighters deserted their Prophet and ran towards the mountain and climbed on a high rock. Being left alone, Muhammad was left with no choice except to run for his life.

When Muhammad was chased by the Makkan fighters he fell in a small ditch and began to shout, "Come to my help you Muslim there, come to me you Muslim there I am the Messenger of Allah, but no one turns to his rescue, while the arrows of the Makkans come to him from every direction" (Ibid: 261). The same incident narrated by al-Tabari as follows "When the Prophet was attacked his friends fled from him. Some of them ran back to Medina and some climbed on a rock on the top of a mountain. Meanwhile, the Prophet continues to call come to me oh servants of Allah, come to my help oh servants of Allah" (Ibid). In that critical moment the Prophet of Islam was beaten badly by the Makkan fighters.

'Atouba ibn Nafi'a was able to reach Muhammad and broke his egg on the head of the Prophet. While Abd Allah ibn Shihab was able to hit the Prophet on his forehead and caused a big cut on it. Ibn Qimah al-Harithi broke his nose and his shoulder. Then, he hit him with his weapon until two parts of it entered the blessed cheek of the Prophet. In all this, the Prophet was calling his friends to come for his help. Then, the Messenger of Allah fell in a ditch when ibn Qimah made a second attack on him and strike his shoulder with full force. However, the two armours protected the Prophet from the strike but he continued to complain from the pain for a full month after Uhud... In that critical moment, the brave warrior, Abu Diganah saw the Messenger of Allah in his desperate condition and ran to him and threw his body on him to protect him. The arrows of the Makkans fell on him until he was killed. At this time, some of the Prophet's friends returned to him and carried him out of the ditch and began to climb the mountain again.

And on a fourth round, the Makkans reached again the place where Muhammad was. When they saw Musa'ad ibn Umiar they thought he was the Prophet. Ibn Qimah mistook Musa'ad for Muhammad and killed him. Then, he ran with his horse towards the unbelievers while he was shouting joyfully **I killed Muhammad'** (Ibid: 261-263, quoting al-Halabi pp 505, 513, al-Tabari pp 519-520, Ibn Kathir p 56, al-Suhaili p 153, and al-Bihaqi p 238).

The shout of Ibn Qimah when he thought he had killed Muhammad was called by all Muslim historians the **'Shout of Satan'** (Ibid: 263). However, that shout al-Qimni believed had rescued the Muslims and their Prophet (Ibid). The battle of Uhud ended with the defeat of Muhammad and his followers. The Makkans ended the battle thinking that Muhammad was killed. Although many Muslims were killed and many more were taken captives, the death of Hamza, the uncle of the

Prophet was great lost for Muslims. Uthman ibn 'Affan was one of those who fled from the battle. According to al-Bihaqi, Uthman and some of his friends ran to "a place called al-Shiqrah which was seventy miles away from Medina. They did not return to Medina until they heard that the Prophet returned to Yathrib with those who remained alive from his followers. Uthman and his friends returned from their hiding place after three days" (Ibid: 272, quoting from al-Bihaqi p. 310).

The Battle of Bani Qurizah: As it is mentioned in the previous chapter that the main reason for the slaughter of the Jewish tribe of Bani Qurizah was to get rid of the last Jewish tribe in Medina. Muhammad accused them that they broke their treaty with him and that by planning to open their garrison for the allied Makkan tribes to attack the Muslims at the Battle of the Ditch. However, as al-Qimni proved that that the Jews were innocent from such an accusation. As a matter of fact Muhammad is the one to be blamed for breaking the treaty. For more details please refer to the previous chapter, under the sub-title **The Slaughter of Banu Qurizah**. However, under this heading we will see how **the Mothers of the Islamic Books** describe how the slaughter took place.

The Prophet said "if anyone hears and obeys should not perform his Asr[59] prayer except in Bani Qurizah'" (Ibid: 391, quoting from al-Tabari al-Tarikh p. 591), Al-Bihaqi narrates that "the Prophet went out and passed by some people of Bani Qurizah and asked them, is there any one passed by you? They said, Dahia al-Kalib[60] passed this way riding on a beautiful horse. The Prophet replied "that is not Dahia but the angel Gabriel, peace be upon him, sent to Bani Qurizah to shake them and put fear in their hearts" (Ibid, quoting from al-Bihaqi, al-Dalail p. 9). Ibn Kathir, al-Tabari, and al-Baihaqi, narrated the dialogue between the Prophet and the frightened Jews of Bani Qurizah jointly as follows:

Muhammad: Oh brothers of monkeys and pigs

The trembling Jews replied: Oh Abu al-Qasim,[61] you have not been a bad man!! (Ibid; 392, quoting from Ibn Kathir, al-Bedayia p. 120).

The Prophet called out to them: Oh brothers of monkeys. Does Allah disappointed you and sent on you his curse?

The Qurizah understood the message and replied in fear: Oh Abi al-Qasim, you have not been an ignorant man (Ibid, quoting from al-Bihaqi, al-Tarikh p. 582).

The Jews of Qurizah continued to plead with Muhammad and beg him to send to them one of their allies, a man by the name of Abi Libabah bin Abd al-Nuziar al-Awasi.

When Abi Libabah entered their garrison, the men rose, the women wept, and the children cried to him. When he saw them he had piety on them.

They said to him: oh Abi Libabah, do you think we should go out for the judgment of Muhammad?

He said, yes, and then he passed his finger across his neck, which means, the slaughter.

Then their leader, Ka'ab bin Asaad said to his people: Let us follow Muhammad and believe in him.

They replied: We will not leave the judgment of the Torah forever.

He said to them: Then let us kill our children and women and go out to Muhammad.

They said: Shall we kill these harmless children and women? What is the good of life after them? (Ibid: 393-394, quoting from al-Tabari p. 583).

Finally the men of Bani Qurizah decided to go out and meet Muhammad hoping that the other Medinian tribes would intercede with the Prophet and request him to send them with their women and children out of Yathrib as he did before with the other two Jewish tribes. As soon as the Jewish men emerged out of their garrison the Prophet ordered his men to bind them with ropes and march them in long que (Ibid: 394, quoting from al-Tabari, al-Tarikh p. 583). Then the Prophet asked his men to dig many ditches inside the city (Ibid). After so many pleadings from the leaders of the Medinian tribes of al-Khariq and al-Awas, Muhammad agreed that Sa'ad bin Mu'aaz should decide the fate of the Jews (Ibid, quoting from al-Tabari p. 586).

Al-Tabari narrated that Sa'ad bin Mu'aaz was dying. During the siege of the city an arrow hit his hand and caused a cut on one of his nerves. The Prophet tried to heal him by heating a nail and burning the nerve. In doing that Muhammad thought the bleeding would stop. However, the burning nail worsened the cut and caused the nerve to swell. When the Prophet repeated the same treatment the nerve exploded (Ibid: 395). In his dying state Sa'ad was carried to the Prophet. When Muhammad saw him he ordered the Jews to stand to their Master. "When Sa'ad was put down by his carriers the Prophet asked him to judge on them. He said, I judge on them that the men should be put to death, their wealth divided, and their women distributed as jawari among the Muslims. The Prophet said to him, **you have judged on them with the judgment of Allah that has been given to you from seven heavens**" (Ibid: 395, quoting al-Tabari, al-Tarikh p. 586, emphasis on the original).

The horrifying slaughter was described by al-Tabari as follows:

They brought first the enemy of Allah, Huaya bin Akhatab,[62] while his hands were bound to his neck by a rope. When Huaya saw the Messenger of Allah, he said to him, I swear by God, I have never blamed myself for your enmity. Then, Huaya turned to the people and said, oh people there is no fear from the judgment and the Book of God, it is an honour written by God to the children of Israel to die as martyrs. Then, he sat down and his neck was beheaded… Ali bin Talib and al-Zibiar continued to strike their necks… It is assumed that their bloods reached the oilstones that are at the market (Ibid: 396, quoting from al-Tabari, al-'Tarikh pp. 588-589).

The narrators of the sira differed in the number of the Jewish men who were killed on that fateful day. Some said six hundred, some seven hundred, some eight hundred, and some nine hundred (Ibid: 396). Al-

Qimni states, "And we learn from our heritage a new thing happened in that **slaughter**. The slaughter was not restricted to men only, but included little boys too" (Ibid: 398 referring to al-Tabari p. 591). Then the victims were buried in those big holes or ditches that the Muslims dug.

According to narrators of the sira, Allah rewarded Sa'ad bin Mu'aaz for his decision and that by dying immediately after the slaughter. The angel Gabriel came to the Prophet in the middle of the night and told him that Sa'ad bin Mu'aaz died and the throne of Allah was shaken in his honour. Moreover, his funeral was attended by seventy thousands angels (Ibid: 397, quoting from al-Bihaqi pp. 28-29). The number of the booty was counted by Ibn Sa'ad as one thousand five hundred swords, three hundred armours, one thousand spears, one thousand and five hundred shields, and many camels and cows. Regarding the women, their number was more than the number of the Muslim men. Therefore, when every Muslim man got his share from the Jewish women, the remaining were sold as slaves to the men of Nagid. Muhammad took Rayhana bint Umaro. Ibn Kathir narrates that, "The Prophet told Rayhana that he would release her from slavery and marry her. However, Rayhana chose to remain in slavery, which she believed more bearable to her... She refused to accept Islam and decided to remain a Jew and slave all her life" (Ibid: 401, quoting Ibn Kathir, al-Bedaya, p. 128 and al-Tabari, al-Tarikh, p. 592).

Men and Women murdered because they criticized Muhammad:

1- **Asma Bint Marwan, of Banu Umayyah Ibn Zayd**: Asma was the wife of Yazid Ibn Zayd Ibn Hisn al-Khatmi. She used to revile Islam, offend the prophet and instigate the (people) against him. She composed verses in which she criticized the Prophet. Muhammad sent Umar ibn Adi to go and kill her. Umar came to her in the night and entered her house. Her children were sleeping around her. There was one whom she was suckling. He searched her with his hand because he was blind, and separated the child from her. He thrust his sword in her chest till it pierced up to her back. Then he offered the morning prayer with the prophet at al-Medina. The apostle of Allah said to him: "Have you slain the daughter of Marwan?" He said: "Yes. Is there something more for me to do?" He [Muhammad] said: "No. Two goats will butt together about her. This was the word that was first heard from the apostle of Allah. The apostle of Allah called him `Umar, "al-basir" (the seeing) (Ibn Sa`d's *Kitab al-Tabaqat al-Kobara,* volume 2, p. 31).

2- **Abu Afak**, a man of great age (reputedly 120 years) was killed because he lampooned Mohammad. The deed was done by Salem b. 'Umar at the behest of the Prophet, who had asked, "Who will deal with this rascal for me?" The killing of such an old man moved a poetess, Asma b. Marwan, to compose disrespectful verses about the Prophet, and she too was assassinated.

3- **Abdullah Ibn Sa'ad Ibn Abi Sarh**: Muhammad had scribes write his revelations down for him. One scribe was `Abdullah Ibn Sa'ad Ibn Abi Sarh. As Sarh wrote these revelations down, he frequently made suggestions on improving their wording. Muhammad often agreed and allowed the changes to be made. Eventually, Sarh left Islam, knowing it could not be from God if a mere scribe were allowed to change God's word. Later, after the conquest of Makka, Muhammad ordered Sarh's death. "A person of al-Ansar had taken a vow to kill Ibn Abi Sarh [the already mentioned Abdullah] if he saw him. Uthman whose foster brother he (Ibn Abi Sarh) was, came and interceded for him with the prophet. The Ansari was waiting for the signal of the prophet to kill him. Uthman interceded and he [Muhammad] let him go. The apostle of Allah said to the Ansari, "Why did you not fulfill your vow?" He said, "O apostle of Allah! I had my hand on the hilt of the sword waiting for your signal to kill him. The prophet said signaling would have been a breach of faith. It does not behave the prophet to make signal (Ibn Sa'ad in *Kitab al-Tabaqat al-Kobara* p. 174).

4- **Kinanah al-Rabi**, who had the custody of the treasure of Banu Nadir, was brought to the apostle who asked him about it. He denied that he knew where it was. A Jew came (Tabari says "was brought"), to the apostle and said that he had seen Kinana going round a certain ruin every morning early. When the apostle said to Kinana, "Do you know that if we find you have it I shall kill you?" He said, "Yes". The apostle gave orders that the ruin was to be excavated and some of the treasure was found. When he asked him about the rest he refused to produce it, so the apostle gave orders to al-Zubayr Al-Awwam, "Torture him until you extract what he has." So he kindled a fire with flint and steel on his chest until he was nearly dead. Then the apostle delivered him to Muhammad bin Maslama and he struck off his head (Ibn Ishaq, *Sirat Rasulallah 'Biography of the Messenger of Allah'* p. 37).

5- **Abdullah Khatal of B. Taym b. Ghalib**. He had become a Muslim and the apostle sent him to collect the poor tax in company with one of the Ansar. He had with him a freed slave who served him. (He was Muslim). When they halted he ordered the latter to kill a goat for him and prepare some food, and went to sleep. When he woke up the man had done nothing, so he attacked and killed him and apostatized. He had two singing-girls Fartana and her friend who used to sing satirical songs about the apostle, so he ordered that they should be killed with him. Khatal was ordered to be killed not because he killed his male slave, a Muslim, but because he apostatized. Islamic law does not allow a Muslim man to be put to death for killing a slave, a Jew, a Christian, or any another non-Muslim. A person came to the Prophet and said, "O apostle of Allah! Ibn Khatal is holding fast the curtains of al-Ka'aba. The apostle of Allah said: "Kill him." The Prophet ordered the two slave girls to be killed for singing satirical songs about him.

The Harlots of Hadramaut: The death of the Prophet Muhammad was celebrated joyfully by twenty-six noble women in Hadramaut, a city in Yemen. Muslim historians called them 'The Harlots of Hadramaut." The celebration is narrated by Ibn Habib al-Baghdadi in his book, "Kitab al-Muhabbar": "There were in Hadramaut six women, of Kinda and Hadramaut, who desired the death of the Prophet of God; they therefore [on hearing the news] dyed their hands with henna and played on the tambourines. To them came out the harlots of Hadramaut and did likewise so that some twenty-odd women joined the six". However, Ibn Habib contradicts his statement that the women were 'Harlots' when he describes them as "Two were grandmothers, one a mother, and seven were young girls. Three of the twelve belonged to the *ashraf* ("the noble class") and four to the tribe of Kindah, a royal tribe which provided Yemen with its kings."

Two Muslim leaders wrote to Caliph Abu Bakr and reported the event. When the news reached the first caliph, Abu Bakr, he wrote back ordering that the hands of the women to be cut off.

> The two righteous servants [of God] who remained steadfast in their religion when the greater part of their tribes apostatized…have written to me that before them there are certain women of the people of Yemen who have desired the death of the Prophet of God, and that these have been joined by singing-girls of Kinda and prostitutes of Hadramaut, and they have dyed their hands and shown joy and played on the tambourine in defiance of God and in contempt of his rights and those of His Prophet. When my letter reaches you, go to them with your horses and men, **and strike off their hands**.

Following the order of the Caliph, the twenty-six women were punished in a gruesome manner and that by having their hands chopped off.

<u>Conclusion</u>: Perhaps the best way to end this book is to quote the concluding paragraph of Muhammad Asghar in his book, *MUHAMMAD & ISLAM: Stories not told before,*

Whatever was the cause of his death, his departure ended a long period of tyranny. His death freed his wives from his bondage; it gave a sigh of relief to the pagans who he forced to abandon their ancestral faith and it also removed the shadow of his omnipresent sword from the heads of the Jews. On the flipside, he left behind a set of religious doctrines, which have been impacting the lives of a vast number of his followers even after his death some 1400 years ago. While some of his teachings have proven instrumental in crippling the lives of many of his own followers, others have been helping them to create schism and hatred in those humans who follow different philosophies of life. Allah-o-Akbar, essentially a Muslim war cry, still turns many Muslims engaged in battles, interfaith riots and sectarian conflicts into ferocious animals; alleged support given in the past by angels to the warring Muslims against the infidels drive small and weaker Islamic States to challenge the combined might of the world's all industrialized nations; murder of the Jews by Muhammad and his hateful teaching against them (5:54) still generate fiery desire in most of the Muslims the elimination of all Jews from the face of planet earth and his call to kill the pagans whenever and wherever they are found (59:5) is a constant source of inspiration for many of his followers to engage themselves in the murder of all the Hindus of the world. His belligerent teachings, as Bernard Lewis has pointed out in his book, "The Crisis of Islam," are considered by many Muslims to be a duty for them to "destroy the entire world before their apocalyptic design of restoring the Islamic caliphate can be realized (Asghar part 13).

Chapter 13 Endnotes

[52] The Land of the Islam.

[53] The land of the War.

[54] Uncle of the Prophet Muhammad and his father-in-law (father of Zainab bint Jahsh). For more detail see the last chapter, Scandalous Marriages of Muhammad.

[55] A list of the Battles of the early Islamic State is given in the next chapter.

[56] Father of the Prophet's wife, Zainab bint Jahash. Please refer to Muhammad's scandalous marriage to Zainab bint Jahsh in chapter twelve.

[57] Shihadah means accepting Islam by saying 'I bear witness that there is no Gob, but Allah and Muhammad is the Messenger of Allah'. This is known as uttering the two witnesses, the first for Allah and the second for Muhammad.

[58] "The People of the Book" are the Jews and Christians.

[59] 'The third prayer of the day.

[60] Dahia al-Kalib was a very handsome young Muslim man. The Prophet claimed that whenever the Angel Gabriel appeared to him he appeared in the form of this handsome young man.

[61] Father of Abu al-Qasim. The Prophet was called by that title because he had a son by that name.

[62] He is the father of Safiya bint Huaya whom the Prophet killed her husband, brother, and father and took her as his wife. For more detail see the last chapter, The Scandalous Marriages of Muhammad.

*References*⁶³

1- Abd al-Gadir, Asharaf Abd al-Fatah, 2004. "The Reformation of Islam is a Duty and Compulsory if we do not want to be the Last Nation emerged," Modern Discussion, Elaph Publication, March 16, 2004, http://www.rezgar.com/debat/show.art.asp?aid=.

2- Abdul-Karim, Khalil, 1999. *The State of Yathrib,* Sinah Lilnashir, First Edtion, Cairo, Egypt.

3- Abdo, Geneive 2002. *No God But God, Egypt and the Triumph of Islam*, New York: Oxford University Press.

4- Afshari, Reza, 1994, *Egalitarian Islam and Misogynist Islamic Tradition: A Critique of the Feminist Reinterpretation of Islamic History and Heritage*, An Easy, Institute for the Secularization of Islamic Society, info@SecularIslam.org

5- Ahmed, Leila. 1992. *Women And Gender In Islam: Historical Roots of a Modern Debate*. New Haven, Yale University Press.

6- al-Akhwan al-Muslimoon, 2004. "A campaign Against the Islamic Identity of Egypt," Muslim Brothers Newspaper, Jan 1, 2004. (Accessed on March 20, 2004). http://www.ikhwanonline.com/Article.asp?ID=4349&SectionID=349 p http://odur.let.rug.nl/~nch/action6.htm#general

7- Annual Report 1997. "Network of Concerned Historians" (NCH # 5 & 6), Source: IOC 4/97: 15, 1997. (Accessed on April, 2005). http://odur.let.rug.nl/~nch/action6.htm#general

8- Asghar, Mohammad, *MUHAMMAD & ISLAM: Stories not told before*: "Freethinkers." http://www.mukto-mona.com/Articles/asghar/muhammad_islam12.htm

9- Ayalon, Ami. 1999. "Egypt's Quest for Cultural Orientation". The Moshe Dayan Center for Middle Eastern and African Studies: Data and Analysis. (Accessed on May 10, 2004) http://www.dayan.org/D&A-Egypt-ami.htm.

10- Balz, Kilian, 1997. "Submitting Faith to Judicial Scrutiny Through the Family Trial: The Abu Zayd Case". Welt des Islamus 37.2 (1997) 135-155.

11- Barlas, Asma, 2002. *Believing Women In Islam: Unreading Patriarchal Interpretations of the Qur'an.* Austin, TX: University of Texas Press.

12- Boyarin, Daniel, 1998. Gender. In *Critical Terms of Religious Studies.* Taylor, Mark C. (ed.) Chicago and London: Chicago University Press.

13- Da'agir, Hamdoon, 2002, The Place of Woman In Islam, 6 November, 2002. <htt://www.geocities.com/aboutchristianity/MAKANT ALMA2A.htm

14- Drucken, English, 2003. "Nasr Hamid Abu Zayd" QUR'ANIC HERMENEUTICS, (Accessed on May 25, 2004), 2002-2003. http://www.wiko-berlin.de/kolleg/fellows/fellows2002-2003/abuzayd

15- Engel, Richard, 1998. "Book Ban Exposes Azhar Censorship," Middle East Times, May 1, 1998, (Accessed on Feb 28, 2004. http://www.dfn.org/voies/egypt/metimes/bookban.htm.

16- *Feminism and Islam,* Legal and Literary Perspectives, 1981, ed., by Yamani, Mai. Publishers: Al-Sabag, M. Mutawali.

17- Feminism In the Study of Religion: a Reader. 2001. Juschka, M. Darlene (editor). London and New York, Continuum.

18- Haddad, Yvonne Yazbeck and Stowasser, Barbara. 1998. Islam and Gender: Dilemmas in the Changing Arab World. In *Islam, Gender, and Social Change*, edited by Yvonne Yazbeck Haddad and John L. Esposito, 1-28, 30-44. New York, Oxford University Press.

19- -------- 1985. Women, *Religion, and Social Change,* edited by Yvonne Yazbeck Haddad and Ellison Banks Findly. State University of New York Press.

20- Haqq, M. Rafiqul & P. Newton, 1996, *The Place of Women in Pure Islam,*. <http://www.debate.domini.org/newton/womeng.html>

21- Hassan, Riffat, 2001, "On Human Rights and the Qur'anic Perspective," pp. 51-65, 9.03, Journal of Ecumenical Studies.

22- --------- "Challenging the Stereotypes of Fundamentalism: An Islamic Feminist Perspective". The Muslim world; a quarterly review of history, culture, religions & the Christian mission in Islamdom. 91, no. 1, (2001).

23- Ismail, Salwa. 2004. "The Politics of Historical Revisionism: New Re-Readings of the Early Islamic Period." In *An Islamic Reformation?* Edited by Michaelle Browers and Charles Kurzman, 101-124. New York, LEXINGTON BOOKS.

24- Kepel, Gilles. 1993. *Muslim Extremism In Egypt: The Prophet and Pharaoh*, Berkeley: University of California Press, 1993, c1985.

25- Kim, Caroline. 2005. "Threats cause Egyptian writer to renounce his life's work" Overseas Press Club of America

26- Lois, Lamya al-Farugi, 1985, <u>Marriage In Islam</u>, pp. 55-68, Vol 22, in Journal of Ecumenical Studies.

27- Mahmoud, Hala and Middle East Times staff, "<u>In Search of what went wrong</u>," <u>Middle East Times,</u> (Accessed on March 21, 2004), <u>http://www.metimes.com/issue11/cens/c3.html,</u> p 1.

28- Mernissi, Fatima, 1987, *Beyond the Veil*, Bloomington and Indianapolis, Indiana University Press.

29- -------- 1988, *Women's Rebellion & Islamic Memory*, Zed Books Ltd.

30- -------- 1993, *Women and Islam, an Historical and Theological Enquiry,* Kali for Women, New Delhi.

31- -------1993. (Mary Jo Lakelan, trans.). *The Forgotten Queens of Islam*, Polity Press, Oxford.

32- the Middle East Media Research Institute September 27, 2004. (Accessed on December 14, 2004). <u>http://www.memri. org/bin/articles.cgi?Page=archives&Area=sd&ID=SP7900 4#_edn4</u>

33- Mills, Sarah. 1997. *Discourse: The New Critical Idiom.* London, New York. Routledge.

34- al-Muhsin, Fatima, 2004. "Arabic Cultures or One Culture" <u>Riyadh Daily Newspaper</u>, Feb 26, 2004. (Accessed on March 23, 2004, <u>http://www.alriyadh-np.com/Contents/26-02-2004/Mainpage/Thkafa_10479.php,</u>

35- Najjar, Fauzi, M. 1996. "The Debate on Islam and Secularism in Egypt" <u>Arab Studies Quarterly</u> 18.2 (1996) 1-21.

189

36- -------- 2000. "Islam's Fundamentalism and the Intellectuals: "The Case of Nasr Hamid Abu Zayd". British Journal of Middle Eastern Studies. 2702 (2000) 177-200.

37- -------- 2001. "Book Banning in Contemporary Egypt" Muslim World 91.3/4 (2001) 399-425.

38- Phillips, Louise & Jorgensen, Marianne W. 2002. *Discourse Analysis: as Theory and Method.* London, SAGE Publications Ltd.

39- al-Qimni, Sayyid Mahmoud 1996. *Al-Hizb Al-Hashmi Wa Tasis Al-Dawla Al-Islamyia (The Hashmite Party and The Foundation of the Islamic State),* Makatabat Madbouli Al-Sageer, Fourth Edition, Cairo, Egypt.

40- -------- 1996. *Rab Al-Zaman (The Lord of Times),* Maktabat Madbouli Al-Sageer, First Edition, Cairo, Egypt.

41- -------- 1999. *Al-Fashoon wa al-Watan (The Fascists and the Nation),* The Egyptian Center for Civilization Researches, First Edition, Cairo, Egypt.

42- ------ 2001. *Hurub Dawlat al-Rasul, (The Wars of the Prophet's State).* Al-Islamiyat (Islamisms), The Egyptian Centre for Civilization Researches, First Edition, Cairo, Egypt.

43- -------- 2004. *Shukran...Bin Laden (Thanks...Bin Laden),* Dar Misr Al-Mahrosa, First Edition, Cairo, Egypt.

44- Saadawi, Nawal. 1981. *The Hidden Face of Eve: Women In the Arab World.* Boston, Beacon Press.

45- -------- 2001, *Women Creativity and Mental Health,* http://www.nawalsaadawi.net/articleby/mental_health.htm,

46- al-Sabaq, M. Mutawli, 1981, <u>Illustrations In Marriage Regulations</u>, Egypt, Madboli Maktaba.

47- al-Samti, Abd Allah, 2004. "Doubtful Writings" <u>Al-Watan</u>, March 15, 2002, Accessed on March 20, 2005, <u>http://www. alwatan.com.sa/daily/2002-03-15/writers/writers24.htm</u>

48- Sarahan, Samir, 2004. "Scribe of the Republic," <u>Egypt Times, 5 February 1998, Vol 2, Iss 25</u> (Accessed on March 20, 2004, <u>http://www.cairotimes.com/content/culture/sarhan.html</u>

49- Sayf al-Islam, Ahmad & el-Gawhary, Karim 1995. "Shari'a or Civil Code? Egypt's Parallel Legal Systems: An Interview with Ahmad Sayf al-Islam" <u>Middle East Report</u> 197 (Nov-Dec 1995) 25-25

50- Sfeir, George N. 1998. "Basic Freedom in a fractured Legal Culture: Egypt and the Case of Nasr Hamid Abu Zayd". <u>Middle East Journal</u> 32.3 (Summer 1998). 402-414.

51- al-Shara'any, Abd Al-Wahhab, 1981, <u>Khashaf Al-Khomah</u>, Beirut (Lebanon), Publishers: Al-Maktabah Al-Alamyyah

52- Sivan, Emmanuel 2003. "The Clash Within Islam" <u>Survival</u> 45.1 (Spring 2003) 25-44.

53- Skovgaard-Petersen, Jakob, 1999. "Defining Islam For the Egyptian State, Muftis and Fatwas of the Dar al-Ifta", <u>Middle East Quarterly</u>, June 1999.

54- Smith Jane & Haddad, Yvonne, 2001, "Women in the Afterlife: The Islamic View as Seen from Qur'an and Tradition," 43.01, pp. 39-50, <u>Journal of the American Academy of Religion.</u>

55- Smith, Jane, I. 2001, <u>Women in Islam: Equity, Equality, and the Search for the Natural Order</u>, XLVII/4, pp. 517-537, Journal of the American Academy of Religion.

56- Strowasser, Barbara, Jan-April, 1992, The Mothers of the Believers in the Hadith, pp. 1-36, Vol LXXXII, Journal of Muslim World.

57- Verma, B. R., 1988, <u>Muslim Marriage, Dissolution, and Maintenance</u>, The Law Book Company (P) Ltd.

58- Wadud, Amina. 1999. *Qur'an and Woman: Rereading the Sacred Text from a Woman's Perspective.* New York, Oxford University Press.

59- Weaver, Mary Anne, 1998. "Revolution By Stealth" <u>New Yorker </u>June 8, 1998.

60- Woodsmall, R. Frances, 1983, *Women In Changing Islamic System,* New Delhi (India), Bimla Publishing House.

61- <u>Women In Cross-Cultural Perspectives</u>, 1991, ed., by Adler, Leomore Leob, New York, Praeger Publishers.

References Endnotes

[63] Works are arranged alphabetically. Works by the same author are arranged chronologically.

The Mothers of the Islamic Books[64]

1- The Holy Qur'an.

2- Sahih Al-Bukhari (collection of the Prophet's sayings).

3- Sahih Muslim (collection of the Prophet's sayings).

4- Sunan Abu Dawud (collection of the Prophet's sayings).

5- Sunan Al-Turmizi (collection of the Prophet's sayings).

6- Ibn al-Atheer, 1965. *Al-Kamil fi Al-Tarikh*. Dar Sadir, Beirut, Lebanon.

7- Al-Asfani. *Al-Agani*. Dar al-Kotob al-Musria, Cairo, Egypt.

8- Al-Awsi. *Ruh al-M'aani*, 12/353.

9- Al-Bihaqi, 1988. *Dalail al-Nobwa*, edited by Abd al-Mu'ati Qaligi, Dar al-Kotob al-'Alimia, Beirut, Lebanon.

10- Ibn Timiah. *Iqitida al-Sirat al-Mustaqim*, Dar al-Mu'arifa, Beirut, Lebano.

11- Tha'alab, 1964. *Shireh Diwan Zuhir*, Al-Dar al-Qumia liltiba'at wa al-Nashir, Cairo, Egypt.

12- Al-Nisaboori, al-Tha'alabi. *Qisas al-Anbia al-Musama 'Arais al-Mugalis,* al-Muktabah al-Thaqafia, Beirut, Lebanon.

13- Ibn al-Gawzi. *Talbos Iblis*, corrected by Muhammad Manir al-Dimishaqi, Al-Mutab'ah al-Munira.

14- Ibn al-Gawzi, Jamal al-Deen, 1985. *Nawasikh al-Qur'an*, Dar al-Kotob al-'Alimia, Beirut, Lebanon.

15- Ibn Habib, 1964. *Al-Munamaq fi Akhabar Qurish,* edited by Khorshid Ahmed Faroq, Daeirat al-Mu'aarif al-Uthmania, Hidar Abad, India. .

16- Al-Halabi. *Al-Sira al-Halabia fi Sirat al-Amin al-Amoon Insaan al-'Uioon,* Dar al-Mu'arifa, Beirut, Lebanon.

17- Ibn Hanabal, 1978. *Kitab al-Zuhud,* Dar al-Kotob al-'Alimiah, Beirut, Lebanon.

18- Ibn Khaldun. *Al-Muqadimah,* Dar al-Sha'ab, Cairo, Egypt.

19- Ibn al-Khiat, Khalifa, 1967. *Al-Tabaqaat,* edited by Akaram al-'Amari, Mutbaat al-Mu'ani, Bagadad, Iraq.

20- Dalo, Burahan al-Deen, 1985. *Musahama fi I'adat Kitabat al-Tarikh al-'Arabi al-Islami,* Al-Farabi, Beirut, Lebanon.

21- Al-Dinoori, 1960. *Al-Akhbaar al-Tiwal,* edited byAbd Al-Mu'anim 'Amir, Wazarat al-Thaqafa wa al-Irishad al-Quami, Cairo, Egypt.

22- Al-Zabadi, 1306 H.[65] *Tag al-'Aroos,* Cairo, Egypt

23- Ibn Sa'ad. *Al-Tabaqaat al-Kubrah,* Dar al-Tahiri li al-Tiba'ah lil al-Nishir, Cairo, Egypt.

24- --------, 1933. *Al-Tabaqaat al-Kabeer,* London print.

25- Al-Sohili, 1978. *Al-Rwad al-Anif fi Tafiseer al-Sira al-Nabawia Libni Husham,* Dar Al-Mu'arifa, Beirut, Lebanon.

26- Ibn Seed al-Naas, 1980. *'Auioon al-Asar fi Finoon al-Mugazi wa al-Shamail wa al-Sira,* edited by lignaat Ihia al-Turath al-'Arabi, Dar al-Afaq al-Gidida, Beirut, Lebanon.

27- Al-Shahristani, 1961. *Al-Milal wa Al-Nahl,* print of al-Babi al-Halabi, edited by Muhammad Said Kilani, Cairo 961 and al-Mutab'a al-Azharia, Cairo 1951, Egypt.

28- Al-Shibani, 1972. *Al-Ikitisaab fi al-Riziq al-Mustatab*, summerized by Muhammad Bin Samah, edited by Muhammad 'Arnoos, Mutabat al-Anwar, Cairo, Egypt.

29- --------, 1972. *Shireh Kitab al-Siar al-Kabeer*, edited by Salahal-Deen al-Mugid, Mu'ahad al-Mukhtootat bi Jamiyat al-Dwal al-'Arabia, Cairo, Egypt.

30- Al-Tabari. *Tarikh al-Rusul wa al-Mulook*, edited by Muhammad Abu al-Fadol, Dar al-Mu'arif, Cairo, Egypt.

31- Al-'Asaqalani,, 1323 H. *Al-Isabah fi Tamiz al-Sahabah*, Mutab'at al-Sa'adah, Cairo, Egypt.

32- Ibn Qitibah, 1969. *Al-Shi'ar wa Al-Shu'arah*, Dar al-Thaqafa, Beirut, Lebanon.

33- --------, 1986. *'Aiuoon al-Akhbar*, al-Kotob al-'Almia, Beirut, Lebanon.

34- Al-Qizwani, Ahmed. *Fagi'at al-Taf*, Mutabat al-Ahram, Kirbila, Iraq.

35- Ibn Kathir, 1988. *Al-Bidaiah wa al-Nihiah*, Dar al-Kotob al-'Alimiah, Beirut, Lebanon.

36- Al-Kilabi, 1924. *Al-Asnaam*, Dar al-Kotob al-Musirish, Cairo, Egypt.

37- Al-Maroodi, 1978. *Al-Ahakam al-Sultania wa al-Wiliat al-Diniah*, Dar al-Kotob al-'Alimiah, Beirut, Lebanon.

38- Al-Maqadisi, 1916. *Al-Bid wa al-Tarikh*, Muktabat al-Muthni, Bagadad, Iraq.

39- Al-Nahas, Abu Ja'afar, 1986. *Al-Nasikh wa al-Munsukh fi al-Qur'an al-Kareem*, edited by Dr. Sha'aban Muhammad Ism'ail, Muktabat "Alam al-Fikir, Cairo, Egypt.

40- Ibn Hisham, 1974. *Al-Sirah al-Nabawia*, edited by Taha Abd Al-R'uf and Muhammad Mahi, Shirikat al-Tiba'ah al-Faniah al-Mutahidah, Cairo, Egypt.

41- Al-Hamadani, 1931. *Al-Aklil*, Bagadad, Iraq.

42- Al-Waqidi, 1966. *Kitab al-Mugazi,* edited by Marisidan Joniz, Minshurat Jamiyat Iksaford, London.

43- Al-Yaqubi, 1974. *Al-Tarikh*, al-Muktabah al-Hidiriah, al-Najaf, Iraq. Abu Yusif, 1979. *Al-Khiraj*, Dar al-Mu'arifa, Beirut, Lebanon.

The Mothers of the Islamic Books Endnotes

64 This list is not comprehensive. However, these are the most authentic and approved Islamic Books.

65 This is an Islamic year.

About the Author

Dr. Ahmed was born in Sudan and earned a PhD in Philosophy from Bombay University, India. He has five University degrees – B. Com., M. A., and PhD in Philosophy from India, and B. A., and M. A., in Philosophy and Religious Studies from Canada. He has a deep concern for the issues of women in Muslim Society.

"The Hidden Life of the Prophet Muhammad" is his ninth book, in which *he reveals hidden things about the life, teachings, and wars of the Prophet Muhammad that you have never heard before.* Accordingly, although many books are written about the life, teachings, and wars of the Prophet Muhammad, however, this book is unique because it reveals things you have never heard before and you are not likely to get them in any other biographies of Muhammad. No matter what religious background you come from, this book is going to change your understanding of Islam and give you better insight into our world today.

Dr. Ahmed has written nine books which all deal with the problems of women in Muslim societies and the hidden causes that led to tragic events such as September 11, and the suicidal missions that going on everyday in the world...

1- Intisar: A Story of a Muslim Girl
2- Insaaf: A Story of an Arab Girl

Dr. Ahmed has a great deal of understanding and experience in his favor because he has viewed the reality of those conditions and causes with his own eyes.

He has a distinctive writing style that breaks through social, religious, and cultural barriers.

CPSIA information can be obtained
at www.ICGtesting.com
Printed in the USA
BVHW072031120620
581302BV00003B/84

9 781425 905712